# APOSTLES TODAY

## C. PETER WAGNER

**Regal**

From Gospel Light
Ventura, California, U.S.A.

Published by Regal Books
From Gospel Light
Ventura, California, U.S.A.
Printed in the U.S.A.

Regal Books is a ministry of Gospel Light, a Christian publisher dedicated to serving the local church. We believe God's vision for Gospel Light is to provide church leaders with biblical, user-friendly materials that will help them evangelize, disciple and minister to children, youth and families.

It is our prayer that this Regal book will help you discover biblical truth for your own life and help you meet the needs of others. May God richly bless you.

*For a free catalog of resources from Regal Books/Gospel Light, please call your Christian supplier or contact us at 1-800-4-GOSPEL or* www.regalbooks.com.

Library of Congress Cataloging-in-Publication Data
Wagner, C. Peter.
  Apostles today / C. Peter Wagner.
     p. cm.
  ISBN 0-8307-4308-1 (hard cover) — ISBN 0-8307-4362-6 (international trade paper)
  1. Apostolate (Christian theology) 2. Christian leadership. 3. Pastoral theology. I. Title.
  BV601.2.W35 2007
  262'.1—dc22                                                                 2006033854

1    2    3    4    5    6    7    8    9    10    /    10    09    08    07

Rights for publishing this book in other languages are contracted by Gospel Light Worldwide, the international nonprofit ministry of Gospel Light. Gospel Light Worldwide also provides publishing and technical assistance to international publishers dedicated to producing Sunday School and Vacation Bible School curricula and books in the languages of the world. For additional information, visit www.gospellight-worldwide.org; write to Gospel Light Worldwide, P.O. Box 3875, Ventura, CA 93006; or send an e-mail to info@gospellightworldwide.org.

# Contents

# CHAPTER ONE

# THE APOSTLES HAVE SURFACED!

**A**re there apostles in our churches today?

Most Christians would affirm that they believe in apostles because Jesus led a group of 12 of them. However, apostles are generally seen as figures of a bygone age, like Vikings, Roman legions, Spanish conquistadors, or pioneers in covered wagons. They made their contributions to history, but the world has moved on.

One reason why this kind of thinking is so prevalent is that this is what most of our church leaders were taught in seminary and Bible school. I know—I was one of them. The notion that there could be contemporary apostles never came up in the seminaries I attended, not even as a suggestion. We were taught that the original 12 apostles had a singular, one-of-a-kind mission that was completed by the time of their deaths, and that was that—the end of the brief life of apostles on Earth. Consequently, I graduated assuming that apostles did not continue long after the first hundred years or so of the Church.

Not so! We are now living in the midst of one of the most epochal changes in the structure of the Church that has ever been recorded. I like to call it the "Second Apostolic Age."

## The Second Apostolic Age

The Second Apostolic Age is a phenomenon of the twenty-first century. My studies indicate that it began around the year 2001. The First Apostolic Age lasted for another 200 years *after* the first of the New Testament apostles concluded their ministry.

This is not to say that the church of Jesus Christ or the kingdom of God went into some kind of hibernation for 1,800 years—it most certainly did not. The true Church has been with us down through the ages, sometimes larger, sometimes smaller, sometimes stronger, sometimes weaker. In Matthew 16:18, Jesus said, "I will build my church," and He has been doing so for over 2,000 years through God's people on Earth as they preach the gospel, make disciples, and set captives free!

## Apostles Throughout History

I have no doubt that apostles have been present in the Church throughout its history. Unfortunately, enemy forces have been busily at work, both in the invisible world and in the visible, trying to keep God's people as subdued as possible. Still, looking back, who could deny that great men such as Gregory Thaumaturgus, Martin of Tours, Patrick of Ireland, Benedict of Nursia, Boniface, Anselm of Canterbury, Savanarola, John Wyclif, Martin Luther, Francis Xavier, John Knox, John Wesley, William Booth, William Carey, Hudson Taylor, and others throughout the centuries were true apostles? A biography of Dwight L. Moody by Wilbur Chapman, published in 1900, even carries the subtitle "A Tribute to the Memory of the Greatest Apostle of the Age."[1]

Calling Moody "an apostle" in 1900 clearly was an exception to the rule. Generally speaking, even those who unquestionably had the gift and ministry of apostle were not publicly recognized by the Church as such. There were a few other notable exceptions, such as the Irvingites of the 1800s and the Apostolic Church of the early 1900s, but they were regarded as mere splinter groups. Historically, apostles were kept beneath the surface after the first couple of centuries or so. But times are changing. A growing number of Christian leaders now recognize, acknowledge and affirm both the gift and the office of apostle in today's churches. The apostles have surfaced!

It took about 100 years to get to where we are now. Four notable movements of the Spirit of God have been building the foundation of the Second Apostolic Age for several decades:

- *The African Independent Churches.* The first churches planted by Western missionaries throughout Africa closely resembled the churches back home in Europe that had sent the missionaries. They looked and functioned much like the churches of the German Lutherans, the British Anglicans, the Swiss Reformed, the New England Congregationals, and others. As the second generation of Christian believers in these churches matured, they became aware of a lack of contextualization in the teachings coming from the pulpit. Consequently, many of them separated from these mission churches of their parents and birthed independent churches that not only put an emphasis on theological context but were also more compatible with African culture. Governmentally, these African Independent Churches were apostolic in nature, although the title "apostle" was not uniformly employed. The subsequent growth of these churches has far outpaced that of the traditional churches of the region.

- *The Chinese House Churches.* The phenomenal Chinese House Church Movement began when Chairman Mao's Cultural Revolution ended in 1975. Over the ensuing decades, the movement has produced an evangelistic harvest of epochal proportions. Some estimate that 10 percent of the Chinese are now believers—in spite of a government that is almost violently anti-Christian. These churches also operate in apostolic government, though they've only recently begun using the title.

- *The Latin American Grassroots Churches.* Around 1980, the growth of the evangelical (a.k.a. Protestant) movement in Latin America began to increase exponentially, due to the emergence of grassroots megachurches in most Latin American metropolitan areas. These churches, of 3,000 to 10,000 members or more, are pastored by individuals who typically have had no personal mentoring from foreign missionaries and have never attended traditional seminaries or Bible institutes. Many of these pastors were called to plant churches while they held positions in the business world. These churches are completely integrated within the Latin American culture and are led apostolically.

• *The U.S. Independent Charismatic Movement.* As an offshoot of the Pentecostal Movement, independent charismatic churches began to multiply in the United States around 1970. One of the major differences between the two was that Pentecostal churches were usually committed to democratically-based church government, whereas independent charismatic churches were apostolic in nature. By the mid-1980s the charismatic churches had become the fastest-growing in America.[2]

## The New Apostolic Reformation

My term for the new wineskin that God has provided for these churches is the "New Apostolic Reformation." It is a "reformation" because we are currently witnessing the most radical change in the way of "doing church" since the Protestant Reformation. It is "apostolic" because the recognition of the gift and office of apostle is the most radical of a whole list of changes from the old wineskin. And it is "new" to distinguish it from several older traditional church groups that have incorporated the term "apostolic" into their official name. (Although it is beyond the scope of this book, those who would like details on the nature of the

significant transitions in church life from the old denominational wineskin to the new apostolic wineskin may consult my book
*Churchquake!* [Ventura, CA: Regal Books, 1999].)

## Scriptural Foundation

If the Spirit has truly been speaking to the churches about the
apostolic wineskin that I am describing in this book, then it is
clearly biblical.

There are three Scripture verses that serve as the primary
proof texts for recognizing the gift and office of apostle. Many
other texts support this, but these three are core: Ephesians 4:11,
Ephesians 2:20, and 1 Corinthians 12:28.

Let's examine each of them.

> And He Himself gave some to be apostles, some proph-
> ets, some evangelists, and some pastors and teachers
> (Eph. 4:11).

As the verse indicates, the five foundational, governmental,
equipping offices are apostle, prophet, evangelist, pastor and
teacher. The "He" is Jesus, who gave these gifts to His people when
He ascended into heaven after rising from the dead and spending
40 days with His disciples (see Eph. 4:8). He subsequently gave
gifted *people* to the Church on two levels: (1) the foundational or
governmental level (see Eph. 4:11), and (2) the ministry level
through the saints (see Eph. 4:12).

A common term for these five offices is "the ascension gifts,"
because Jesus first gave them at His ascension. Many people refer
to them as "the fivefold ministry." However, this may not be the
best term, because "ministry" is not mentioned in verse 11 but in
verse 12, as the role of all of the saints, while apostles, prophets,

evangelists, pastors and teachers are those who *equip* the rest of the saints to do their ministry. This may seem like a minor point, but it is the reason I refer to the five ascension gifts as "foundational" or "governmental" or "equipping" offices.

> [The household of God, i.e., the church, is] built on the foundation of the apostles and prophets, Jesus Christ Himself being the chief cornerstone (Eph. 2:20).

A well-known hymn states that "the church's one foundation is Jesus Christ her Lord." This is obviously true in a general, theological sense because there would be no Church at all without the Person and work of Jesus Christ. However, in the nuts and bolts of the growth and development of the Church after He ascended and left the earth, Jesus apparently prefers to be thought of not as the *foundation* but as the *cornerstone*. The foundation of the Church through the ages is to be made up of apostles and prophets. The cornerstone is essential because it is the primary building block, the identifying, central stone that holds the foundation together and guides the laying of all subsequent blocks that go into constructing the building. If a church has Jesus *without* apostles and prophets, it has no foundation from which to initiate solid building. The two go hand in hand; there cannot be one without the other.

The wording of this verse—"built on the foundation"—is another reason why I call apostles, prophets, evangelists, pastors and teachers the "foundational" offices.

> And God has appointed these in the church: first apostles, second prophets, third teachers, after that miracles, then gifts of healings, helps, administrations, varieties of tongues (1 Cor. 12:28).

The numbers in the verse, *proton* (first), *deúteron* (second), and *tríton* (third), indicate that this not simply a random selection of gifts and offices. *Proton* in this instance should be interpreted to mean that apostles are first in order or sequence, not necessarily in importance or hierarchy. Hierarchy is an old-wineskin concept. To put it simply, a church without apostles will not function as well as a church with apostles.

The traditional Protestant Church has understood apostles and prophets to be offices relegated to the First Apostolic Age but not continuing in churches throughout history. Based on that understanding (that there are no longer apostles and prophets in our churches), then teachers, who are next in line according to 1 Corinthians 12:28, would now be first in order. Obviously, this is not so.

Protestant denominationalism over the past 500 years has been, for the most part, governed by teachers and administrators, rather than by apostles and prophets. That means that denominational executives are actually administrators—good, godly and wise ones, but administrators nonetheless. Most pastors of local churches are assumed to be teachers (at least ever since the sermon became the central point of weekly congregational gathering), with the sermon being their primary vehicle for teaching their people.

It is fascinating that even though we have had church government backward over the past two centuries according to 1 Corinthians 12:28, we have evangelized so much of the world! Think of what will happen now that church government is getting in proper order. Administrators and teachers are essential for good church health and will function much better once the apostles and prophets are in place.

A major stumbling block in the minds of many who first hear this news of the Second Apostolic Age has been the assumption that once the apostles and prophets completed their work of laying the foundation of the Church in the first couple of centuries, that ended the divine assignment of apostles on Earth—as if they were no longer needed. This deeply entrenched notion cannot be biblically sustained, however, given the statement of Ephesians 4:11. After saying that Jesus gave to the Church apostles, prophets, evangelists, pastors and teachers for the equipping of the saints for the work of the ministry, the length of time they would be needed is then stated: "*Until* we all come to the unity of the faith and the knowledge of the Son of God, to a perfect man, to the measure of the stature of the fullness of Christ" (Eph. 4:13). Who in their right mind can claim that we have arrived at that point? The only reasonable conclusion is that we are still in need of all five offices.

## Post-World War II Apostles

In North America, God began to open doors for the emergence of the apostles of the Second Apostolic Age right after World War II. It was around that time when some churches began to recognize the office of apostle. However, the movement eventually sputtered. During those days, terms such as "Latter Rain," "Restorational Movement," "Deliverance Evangelism" and "Shepherding Movement" were used, to name a few. The leaders of those movements had great expectations that what they had started would reform the entire Church in their generation. But it didn't happen. The majority of those post-World War II movements of God no longer exist today; and those that do, have relatively little influence.

However, the leaders of these movements were true pioneers. Their post-World War II apostolic movements were clearly initiated by God Himself. And they were glorious! Huge numbers were saved, healed, delivered, discipled, sent out as missionaries, and personally revived. But many of the pioneers who led the movements made their share of mistakes. We shouldn't see that as strange. Making mistakes goes with the territory of being a pioneer. Think of the pioneers who opened up the western United States. They made their share of mistakes as well. They killed too many buffalo. They broke promises they had made to the Indians. They ruined good farmland. But with all their mistakes, our pioneers laid the groundwork for what the United States is today, and we take off our hats to them. But let's also take off our hats to the Christian leaders of 50 years ago! They were true pioneers who began to shape the new wineskins that we are blessed with today in the Body of Christ.

It has been acknowledged that one of the handicaps of the post-World War II apostolic movement was that the way for the apostles had not been adequately opened for them by the intercessors and prophets. Apostles without proper connections to gifted intercessors and prophets can never be all that God desires them to be.

## Intercessors, Prophets and Apostles

While their post-World War II efforts may have sputtered, they did not die. In the early 1990s, God began once again to speak to the Church about restoring the office of apostle. This time the process was different. It was a bit more gradual, involving first the office of intercessor and then the office of prophet, in order to pave the way for the apostles.

The decade of the 1970s saw the beginnings of the emergence of the enormous global prayer movement that we see today. It was during that process when the Body of Christ began to accept the gift and office of intercessor. In the 1970s and 1980s, it was still unusual—even odd—for churches to recognize certain members as "our intercessors." But no longer. It is the rare church today, even among most denominational churches, that does not recognize intercessors.

Then, during the 1980s, the gift and office of prophet began to surface in churches. Not that prophets had been absent in previous years and centuries, but now their ministry was being understood by a much wider segment of the Body of Christ. The prophets gained stature in the 1990s, and their ministry is now broadly acknowledged and appreciated.

Looking back, I think that we can discern God's logic in bringing intercessors and prophets on the scene before apostles. The role of intercessors is essentially to stand in the gap and open the communication highways between heaven and Earth. Once they are open, the voice of God can be heard more clearly. Although we can all hear from God, the prophets are the most specifically designated individuals to hear God's voice. It is their role to receive and make known the divine messages directed to God's people. But most prophets will themselves admit that they have little idea of what to do with most of the words they receive. It is the apostles, working hand in hand with prophets, who have the task of setting in order and implementing what God wants done on Earth in a certain season.

## A New Assignment for the Twenty-first Century

I am writing about these pioneering efforts through hearsay, as I did not experience them firsthand. While I have been in ordained Christian ministry since 1955, the traditional evangelical circles that I previously moved in knew virtually nothing about the apostles and healing evangelists of those days. The brief references to them that I heard from my seminary professors in the early 1950s relegated them to the lunatic fringe. I really didn't tune in strongly to the apostolic movement until 1993 when I received a clear, new assignment from God to raise apostolic ministry to the top of my personal agenda.

It took me until 1999—the eve of the twenty-first century—to publish *Churchquake!* That's not too long ago!

Which brings us to the matter of timing. The last half of the twentieth century, which began immediately after World War II, is less than 3 percent of all of Christian history! And the time since the reemergence of the idea of apostolic church government in the beginning of the 1990s is only one-half of 1 percent of the history of the Church! The Second Apostolic Age is in its infancy, yet it is already very strong. The movement is not just some fad; it's a move of God! How exciting to be a participant in this revolutionary new season, to find ourselves literally at the hinge point of history!

## Some Disagree

There are some who disagree with this assessment. Back in the pioneer post-World War II days, many highly respected Christian leaders took strong public positions against the fledgling apostolic movement. Whenever the apostolic leaders would make one of their higher profile mistakes—and some of them admittedly did not finish well—their opponents were more than ready to jump up and say, "I told you so!" I strongly suspect that the major reason why the post-World War II movements did not carry the day was that the criticism, which was mostly based on empirical observations, was too strong to overcome.

Even today we find continuing criticism of the New Apostolic Reformation. Take, for example, Vinson Synan. Few would deny that Synan is today's number one historian of the Pentecostal/charismatic movement. His book, *The Century of the Holy Spirit*, is a landmark publication. My high esteem of Synan is precisely what leads me to choose him as a contemporary representative of the opposing view. Here is what he wrote: "It is axiomatic to say that anyone who claims to be an apostle probably is *not* one. An apostle is not self-appointed or elected by any ecclesiastical body, but is chosen by the Lord Himself."[3]

The U.S. Assemblies of God, one of today's most highly respected Christian bodies, is even stronger than Synan in their opposition to the New Apostolic Reformation. During the post-World War II phase, their General Council in 1949 decreed that "The teaching that the Church is built on the foundation of present-day apostles and prophets" is "erroneous."[4] This was reiterated in their General Council of 2000 when the denomination declared that the "teaching that present-day offices of apostles and prophets should govern church ministry" is a "departure from Scripture" and a "deviant teaching."[5]

## Will This Movement Sputter?

I cite these criticisms to raise the question as to whether the current apostolic movement is in danger of sputtering like the last one did. I don't believe it will, based on four observations:

- We have learned from the mistakes of the pioneers, and we are determined not to repeat them. In my personal interaction with large numbers of contemporary apostles, I have every indication that this is a new breed of Christian.

- This movement was preceded by the ministry of intercessors and prophets, who are now part of its shaping and development. Today we have numerous excellent books on intercession and prophecy. During the post-World War II movement, there were practically none.

- The growing library of substantial books on different aspects of apostolic ministry that began to appear in the late 1990s is highly impressive. Many authors are building a solid biblical, historical and theological foundation for the movement. God has revealed (and continues to reveal) insights that the pioneers never had.

• Apostolic accountability has been heightened by the formation of many units of apostles who are holding themselves accountable to peers for their ministry and their character. (More about this later.)

God has given His church the new wineskin of the New Apostolic Reformation, and He will be pouring out new wine into that wineskin for a long time to come!

**Notes**

1. J. Wilbur Chapman, *The Life and Work of Dwight L. Moody: Presented to the Christian World as a Tribute to the Memory of the Greatest Apostle of the Age* (Chicago: J.S. Goodman & Co., 1900).
2. For more information, see "Church Growth" by C. Peter Wagner in *Dictionary of Pentecostal and Charismatic Movements*, Stanley M. Burgess and Gary B. McGee, eds. (Grand Rapids, MI: Zondervan Publishing House, 1988), pp. 180-195.
3. Vinson Synan, "Who Are the Modern Apostles?" *Ministries Today*, March-April 1992, p. 47.
4. 1949 Minutes of the General Council of the Assemblies of God, Resolution 7: "The New Order of the Latter Rain."
5. "Endtime Revival—Spirit-Led and Spirit-Controlled: A Response Paper to Resolution 16," Adopted by General Presbytery, The General Council of the Assemblies of God, August 11, 2000, p. 2.

# CHAPTER TWO

# WHAT APOSTLES DO

How do you know if someone is really an apostle? Because they are doing the work of an apostle! Having said that, however, many still wonder if a certain person who goes by the name of "Apostle So-and-so" really is an apostle.

The problem is, those who don't believe in contemporary apostles are not the only ones who are asking this question. I have heard apostles themselves ask it about other apostles! It is legitimate to wonder how anyone can really know that someone else is a true apostle, but if we can't find a way to agree on a satisfactory answer to that question, then the New Apostolic Reformation will find itself on shaky ground.

Notice how we never hear people ask, "Is so-and-so really a pastor?" Or, "Is so-and-so really a teacher?" Or even, "Is so-and-so really an evangelist?" After all, pastors and teachers and evangelists are just as much a part of Ephesians 4:11 as apostles and prophets. I believe the answer revolves around three factors:

## Comfort Zones

The first has to do with our comfort zones. Most believers today are more comfortable with teachers and pastors and evangelists than they are with the idea of apostles and prophets. Why is this the case? Because the concept of contemporary apostles and prophets is so relatively new that its unfamiliarity challenges the status quo.

Historically, there was probably never a time when there were no teachers in the churches of the world. Teachers have been with us since the First Apostolic Age. Pastors, however, came into their own only at the time of the Protestant Reformation when they replaced the Old Testament office of "priest," which had crept back into the Church. We've had pastors around for 500 years or so; we are well accustomed to them. Evangelists, however, only began to emerge around the mid 1800s, in the days of Charles Finney. The 150 years since then has been plenty enough time to make us quite comfortable with the office of evangelist. Several denominational publications, for example, regularly include a list of their official "evangelists" without anyone raising an eyebrow. Few would question whether Billy Graham, Reinhart Bonnke and Luis Palau are evangelists.

It is not surprising that, since the notion that God is actually raising up prophets and apostles in the Church today is less than 20 years old, many would still feel uncomfortable when they hear about it. The good news is that more and more leaders have now started moving in the direction of affirming the validity of the offices of prophet and apostle. In fact it is worth noting that among the segment of the Body of Christ that could be referred to as "charismatically inclined evangelicals," recognition of the offices of apostle and prophet has become official. In January 2004, Strang Communications convened a consultation of 50 to 60 high-level Pentecostal, Charismatic and apostolic leaders to discuss the issue. The forthcoming "Orlando Statement" says, "We affirm that there is an ongoing post-New Testament activity of the *charismata* of 1 Corinthians 12, as well as the ministries of pastor, teacher, and evangelist described in Ephesians 4. Therefore, it would naturally follow that we affirm the ongoing post-New Testament activity of apostles and prophets."[1]

## Personal Wounding

The second reason why some raise questions as to whether those who use the term "apostle" are legitimate goes back to personal wounding. In the previous chapter I mentioned that our post-World War II pioneer apostles made some unfortunate mistakes. A ripple effect of some of those mistakes turned out to be the emotional damage that many individuals and families experienced who had been caught up in a structure they found to be overly authoritarian, coercive and manipulative. Their disillusionment with some of the apostolic leaders of the time has, not surprisingly, carried over to today. Fortunately, the wounds of many of them have been healed and they are moving on. Furthermore, a new generation is now coming on the scene that does not tend to equate apostolic leadership with personal abuse, as some of their parents may have done.

It should go without saying that the burden of proof that apostolic leadership in the Second Apostolic Age is not repeating the abuses of the earlier movement is squarely on those who are recognized as apostles today. In fact, the issue of apostolic character and integrity is so crucial that I include an entire chapter on it later in this book.

## Apostolic Authority

The third reason why the question, "Is so-and-so an apostle?" is a legitimate one relates to the extraordinary authority resident in a bona fide apostle. The matter of apostolic authority is so important that it warrants a detailed explanation.

Apostles are as different from other members of the Body of Christ as eyes or ears or lungs are from other members of the human body. What is it that makes them different? While there are several things that distinguish apostles from other members of the Body of Christ, the major characteristic that stands out over the others is their exceptional authority. This is reflected in 1 Corinthians 12:28: "And God has appointed these in the church: *first* apostles, second prophets, third teachers" (emphasis added). Thus, apostles are first in the divine order of church leadership.

In my book *Churchquake!*, I describe how churches operate in the New Apostolic Reformation as compared to traditional denominations, and I point out that by far the major difference between the two is "the amount of spiritual authority delegated by the Holy Spirit to individuals."[2] The two operative words in that statement are "authority" and "individuals."

## Where Is the Trust?

In traditional denominations, the locus of authority is ordinarily found in groups, not in individuals. That is why we are accustomed to hearing about deacon boards, boards of trustees, presbyteries, general assemblies, and so on. In the New Apostolic Reformation, however, trust has shifted from groups to individuals. On the local church level, the pastor now functions as the *leader* of the church instead of as an *employee* of the church. On the translocal level, the apostle is the one who has earned the trust of the pastors and other leaders; and trust inevitably imparts authority.

The apostle Paul had no inhibitions about asserting his apostolic authority. For example, back in his days there were some members of the church in Corinth who were asking, "Is Paul really an apostle?" He responded by informing them that not only did he have apostolic authority, but that he would even *boast* about it. "For even if I should boast somewhat more about our authority, which the Lord gave us for edification and not for your destruction, I shall not be ashamed" (2 Cor. 10:8).

Where does this extraordinary authority come from? I go into quite a bit of detail on this in some of my other books, but I want to summarize here the five major sources of apostolic authority:

1. *Apostles have a spiritual gift.* There is such a thing as the spiritual gift of apostle. Part of this gift is strong influence. Knowing that they are apostles because God has chosen to give them the gift of apostle obviously provides apostles a solid foundation of

authority. (In chapter 4 I will elaborate more on understanding and activating spiritual gifts.)

2. *Apostles have an assignment or a call.* All apostles have the gift of apostle, but not all have the same assignment. Apostles who know their God-given ministry assignment know that they are in the will of God. That frees them to move in authority. (This too will be detailed in chapter 4.)

3. *Apostles have extraordinary character.* They have met the requirement that a church leader be "blameless" (see 1 Tim. 3:2). I'll say more about this in the next chapter, but there is no doubt that holiness of character generates authority.

4. *Apostles have followers.* The chief external validation that an individual has the gift of apostle is that others recognize this and willingly submit to the apostle's authority. *No followers, no apostle!* As the old saying goes, "If you think you're leading but nobody is following, then you're probably just out for a walk."

5. *Apostles have vision.* Apostles, when correctly related to prophets, receive revelation from God and consequently are able to say, "This is what the Spirit is saying to the churches right now." Making such a statement with credibility carries with it tremendous authority.

## Self-Appointed Apostles

Vinson Synan was right when he said, "An apostle is not self-appointed or elected by any ecclesiastical body, but is chosen by the Lord Himself." In fact, the term "self-appointed apostle" turns out to be a semantic oxymoron, since no valid apostle is self-appointed any more than valid pastors or teachers are self-appointed. There are false apostles and false pastors and false teachers out there who may be self-appointed, but in this book I address only *true* apostles, not false ones.

God's decision to make an individual an apostle must be recognized and affirmed by real people. If someone says, "God has called me to be an apostle," but no one else agrees, then I have to doubt whether that person has accurately heard from God.

There are those who hear God. For example, the Corinthians did not vote Paul in as an apostle. When he wrote to them, he clearly stated that his authority was given to him by the Lord Himself (see 2 Cor. 10:8). On that point let me make a strong statement: *To the degree that the Corinthian believers did not recognize that the Lord had made Paul an apostle, they were out of the will of God!* That would have been a dangerous place to be!

## Gift vs. Office

There is a crucial difference between the gift of apostle and the office of apostle. They are not the same. The spiritual gift, whether it is the gift of apostle or any other gift, is given to a person through God's grace and by His choice. The Greek word for "grace" is *charis*, which is a part of the word *charisma*, which means "spiritual gift." All gifts are grace-gifts.

However, while the gift is received by the *grace* of God, the office is received through *works*. Furthermore, the office is not given to us by God; it is conferred on us by people. The key indicator in conferring upon someone the office of apostle is the fruit of the gift, as outward evidence that the person actually has the gift. The office becomes the public affirmation that an individual is recognized as having a spiritual gift and that they are authorized to exercise that gift within the Body of Christ. It is important to note that there are a number of people to whom God has given gifts, but who have not entered into their destiny because they have not yet earned their office.

The office of apostle is conferred by responsible people. When asking the question, "Is so-and-so an apostle?" one of the follow-up questions needs to be, "Who else recognizes this person as an apostle?" Those who follow the apostle as subordinates have a significant role in this recognition; but even more important is the affirmation of apostolic peers. This is one of the reasons why apostles are now spontaneously gathering together in peer-level associations of one kind or another, such as the International Coalition of Apostles (ICA), an organization designed to connect as many peer-level apostles with each other as possible. When this happens, there is a much broader mutual recognition of apostolic offices, thereby raising the credibility of contemporary apostolic ministry in general.

At times, an apostle might call upon apostolic peers who have agreed that he or she has the gift of apostle, in order to set them into the apostolic office in a public ceremony. As a part of the maturing process of the apostolic movement, this is happening more frequently. Most apostles are now in agreement that this act should be referred to as "commissioning," not as "ordination." A reason for this is that the candidate has presumably gone through a previous public ceremony of *ordination* in their Christian ministry. Consequently, this new action would be the *commissioning* of an already-ordained minister to a different office.

## Defining "Apostle"

A curious fact is that, in all of the recent literature that has been published on the gift and office of apostle, very few of the authors have offered a finely tuned definition of "apostle." The most complete discussion of different approaches to a definition is found in David Cannistraci's *Apostles and the Emerging Apostolic Movement.* Cannistraci's definition is: "An apostle [is] one who is called and sent by Christ to have the spiritual authority, character, gifts and abilities to successfully reach and establish people in Kingdom truth and order, especially through founding and overseeing local churches."[3] Harold Eberle's definition is more concise: "A true apostle is a minister sent by God to accomplish a specific work."[4]

This is my fifth book relating to apostles. In none of the first four did I offer a definition of apostle. One of the reasons is that I was on such a rapid learning curve that I sensed intuitively that any definition I came up with would probably soon have to be revised—perhaps many times over! Subsequently, however, I have been able to craft a definition that is beginning to stand the test of time and has been accepted as the official definition of the International Coalition of Apostles:

> An apostle is a Christian leader, gifted, taught, commissioned, and sent by God with the authority to establish the foundational government of the church within an assigned sphere of ministry by hearing what the Spirit is saying to the churches and by setting things in order accordingly for the growth and maturity of the church and for the extension of the kingdom of God.

I have attempted, as far as possible, to make this a barebones definition of apostle. My hope is that it clearly sets forth the non-negotiable, essential qualities of all apostles, regardless of what specific apostolic assignment God may have given to each one of them.

## What Apostles Do

There are 12 ministries that we can expect of all apostles. They won't all perform them the same way or to the same degree, but they will be characterized by these activities:

- *They receive revelation.* Apostles hear what the Spirit is saying to the churches. Some of this revelation comes directly to them, some of it is received together with prophets, and at other times through proper relationships with prophets.

- *They cast vision.* An apostle's vision is based on the revelation he or she receives.

- *They birth.* Apostles are self-starters who begin new things.

- *They impart.* God uses apostles to activate His blessings in others (see Rom. 1:11).

- *They build.* Apostles strategize and find ways to carry a project along its intended course, including any funding that may be required.

- *They govern.* Apostles are skilled in setting things in order. Along with prophets, they lay the biblical foundation of the Kingdom (see Eph. 2:20).

- *They teach.* Early believers "continued steadfastly in the apostles' teaching" (see Acts 2:42).

- *They send.* Apostles send out those who are equipped to fulfill their role in expanding the kingdom of God.

• *They finish.* Apostles are able to bring a project or a season of God to its desired conclusion. They are uneasy until the project is done. They seldom burn out.

• *They war.* Apostles are the generals in the army of God. They lead the church in spiritual warfare.

• *They align generations.* Apostles have a long-range perspective on the purposes of God, and they raise up second-tier leadership for the future. Another way of saying this is that they father or mother children in the faith. "For though you might have ten thousand instructors in Christ, yet you do not have many fathers" (1 Cor. 4:15). An excellent resource for this point is Larry Kreider's book *The Cry for Spiritual Fathers and Mothers.*

• *They equip.* Ephesians 4:12 says that apostles equip the saints for the work of the ministry.

## However, Apostles Are Different

It is very important to keep in mind that apostles are not all the same. Watchman Nee makes an interesting observation concerning three of the best known early apostles: Peter, Paul and John. He points out that the differences among the three do not make them opposed to one another, but complementary to each other. Nevertheless, they were different. Peter's primary task, for example, was to be a breakthrough person, one to cast a net into the sea, a pioneer, an evangelist. Paul, while he did some of that as well, was essentially a builder, making known the mystery of Christ, bringing believers to the fullness of their destiny, and setting churches in order. John came later when nominalization and error had begun threatening the Church. He was a restorer, bringing God's people back to a position they had lost.

Watchman Nee says, "We have Peter, concerned first with the ingathering of souls; we have Paul, the wise master builder; and then, when failure threatens, we have John introduced to reaffirm that there is an original purpose still in view, and one that, in the mind of God, has never been abandoned. . . . The practical point of what we have been saying is this, that it takes these three complimentary and interrelated ministries to make the Church perfect."[5]

It is precisely because apostles are different from one another that I am reluctant to expand the definition of apostle to include many common apostolic qualities that some true apostles might not share with each other.

In addition to what apostles do, there are 12 characteristics that are displayed by many (if not most) apostles—though not by all. Some might argue that certain of the items on my list should be included in the definition itself, inferring that an individual who did not score high on that particular item should not be considered an apostle. I respect that point of view, and it's possible they might be right. However, my conclusion at the moment is that none of these characteristics should be considered the final litmus test for answering the question posed in this chapter, "Is so-and-so really an apostle?"

The following twelve biblical characteristics are collective building blocks in the process of apostles "setting things in order," which is part of the basic definition of apostle:

1. *Seeing Jesus personally.* Of course the original 12 saw Jesus, but so did Paul, when Jesus appeared to him on the Damascus Road, and as he indicated in 1 Corinthians 9:1: "Am I not an apostle? Am I not free? Have I not seen Jesus Christ our Lord?" According to an

informal survey of the apostles whom I know today, about 20 percent have actually seen Jesus personally.

2. *Performing supernatural manifestations such as signs and wonders.* "Truly the signs of an apostle were accomplished among you with all perseverance, in signs and wonders and mighty deeds" (2 Cor. 12:12). Almost every apostle I know has seen physical healing in their ministry, but not many have seen mass healings through the casting of their shadow as did Peter (see Acts 5:15). The application of this, therefore, might well be mostly a matter of degree.

3. *Planting churches.* "According to the grace of God which was given to me, as a wise master builder I have laid the foundation and another builds on it" (1 Cor. 3:10). While planting churches is a very important apostolic characteristic (one that David Cannistraci even included in his definition above), not all apostles have a church-planting ministry.

4. *Appointing and overseeing local church pastors (or "elders").* Paul and Barnabas planted churches, and then returned and "appointed elders in every church, and prayed with fasting" (Acts 14:23). Paul instructed Titus, a member of his apostolic team in Crete, to "set in order the things that are lacking, and appoint elders in every city" (Titus 1:5).

5. *Settling disputes in the church.* The Corinthian believers were at each other's throats. Paul wrote, "Now I plead with you, brethren, by the name of our Lord Jesus Christ, that you all speak the same thing, and

that there be no divisions among you, that you be perfectly joined together in the same mind and the same judgment" (1 Cor. 1:10). Apostles are frequently called upon to bring resolution and unity to division.

6. *Applying discipline, including excommunication.* "It is actually reported that there is sexual immorality among you, and such sexual immorality as is not even named among the Gentiles—that a man has his father's wife! . . . In the name of our Lord Jesus Christ, when you are gathered together, along with my spirit, with the power of our Lord Jesus Christ, deliver such a one to Satan for the destruction of the flesh, that his spirit may be saved in the day of the Lord Jesus" (1 Cor. 5:1,4-5). Denominational pastors are rarely equipped to take this kind of drastic action. Apostles, however, have few inhibitions about doing it when needed. Sadly, I have found it necessary through the years to dismiss or to force the resignation of several members of ICA.

7. *Providing spiritual covering for other leaders.* Paul did this. Here are two examples: "I commend to you Phoebe our sister, who is a servant of the church in Cenchrea, that you may receive her in the Lord in a manner worthy of the saints, and assist her in whatever business she has need of you" (Rom. 16:1-2). And, "Now if Timothy comes, see that he may be with you without fear; for he does the work of the Lord, as I also do. Therefore, let no one despise him. But send him on his journey in peace" (1 Cor. 16:10-11).

8. *Suffering physical persecution.* "For I consider that I am not at all inferior to the most eminent apostles . . . From the Jews five times I received forty stripes minus one. Three times I was beaten with rods; once I was stoned; three times I was shipwrecked; a night and a day I have been in the deep" (2 Cor. 11:5,24-25).

9. *Attracting and distributing financial resources.* "All who were possessors of lands or houses sold them, and brought the proceeds of the things that were sold, and laid them at the apostles' feet; and they distributed to each as anyone had need" (Acts 4:34-35). Most apostles have access to the financial resources necessary to implement the vision that God has given them.

10. *Casting out demons.* "So that even handkerchiefs or aprons were brought from [Paul's] body to the sick, and the diseases left them and the evil spirits went out of them" (Acts 19:12). Not all apostles have deliverance ministries, though many do.

11. *Breaking curses of witchcraft.* Paul broke the spirit of divination (witchcraft) in Philippi (see Acts 16:16-18) and directly confronted the occult sorcerer Elymas in Cyprus (see Acts 13:8-11).

12. *Frequent fasting.* As he displays his credentials as an apostle, Paul mentions that he fasted often (see 2 Cor. 11:27).

As we read these lists of what we may expect from apostles, we realize that the requirements for true apostolic ministry are formidable. As Jesus said in Luke 12:48, "To whom much is given, from him much will be required."

## Character: The *Sine Qua Non*

This chapter will go a long way to help us know how we should approach the question, "Is so-and-so really an apostle?" However, none of the multiple forms of ministry we've examined can substitute for a pure heart!

**Notes**

1. "The Orlando Statement," *Ministries Today*, March-April 2004, p. 63.
2. C. Peter Wagner, *Churchquake!* (Ventura, CA: Regal Books, 1999), p. 75
3. David Cannistraci, *Apostles and the Emerging Apostolic Movement* (Ventura, CA: Regal Books, 1996), p. 29.
4. Harold R. Eberle, *The Complete Wineskin* (Yakima, WA: Winepress Publishing, 1993), p. 26.
5. Watchman Nee, *What Shall This Man Do?* (Fort Washington, PA: Christian Literature Crusade, 1961), p. 18.

# CHAPTER THREE

# CHARACTER COUNTS!

Most apostles govern, plant churches, see Jesus, suffer physical persecution, minister in signs and wonders, and perform the duties as listed in the previous chapter. However, what would you think if I said, "Not all apostles exhibit exemplary character"?

That would set off flashing red lights and alarm bells in your mind! How could a person with notable character flaws expect others to follow their leadership? What peer-level apostles would affirm or commission someone who is living a life that does not meet God's standards of behavior?

## Apostle Paul's Chief Sign

When I write about apostles, I find myself quoting 1 and 2 Corinthians quite frequently. The main reason why those two New Testament books contain so much information about apostles is because there was a group of believers in the church at Corinth who were aggressively denying that Paul was really an apostle. As you can well imagine, that did not sit well with Paul, and he strongly defended his apostleship in both letters. In fact, he was so upset that from time to time he even said things that he probably would not have said if he were a bit more calm and collected. Because of this, these two epistles provide us with inside information on apostles and apostolic ministry that we might not otherwise have.

One of the places where Paul defends his apostleship is in 2 Corinthians 12:12, where he says, "Truly the signs of an apostle were accomplished among you with all perseverance, in signs and wonders and mighty deeds." As we have seen, signs and wonders are common among apostles. But in this particular statement, Paul lists a *character* trait—perseverance—before mentioning signs and wonders.

"Perseverance" is translated "patience" in the *King James Version*. The word "patience" has a deeper meaning than, for example, the proper attitude when you find yourself in a long, slow line in the supermarket. David Cannistraci defines it as "remaining persistent in the face of opposition" and "staying anchored when everything around is getting off course."[1] When we look at a person for the purpose of evaluating whether or not he or she might be a true apostle, character questions must come first. I repeat, character is, above all other qualifications, the *sine qua non* for apostolic ministry!

Bill Hamon agrees. He says, "The new breed of apostles will be motivated by the spirit of wisdom. . . . They will minister in the faith that works by love. . . . Their character will be in line with the fruit of the Holy Spirit. . . . Their attitudes, actions, and relationships with others will be according to the attributes of agape-love as revealed in First Corinthians 13."[2]

I also like the way David Cannistraci puts it: "Signs, wonders and mighty deeds have their place to be sure, but having those graces and abilities in operation without the presence of character would be useless as well as harmful." He concludes, "Apostleship is a matter of character above any other single quality."[3]

## Passing the Biblical Tests

The apostles whom I know well enough personally to form an evaluation of their character all pass the biblical tests. I am not surprised by this. In fact, it is exactly what I would expect. A person cannot be a true apostle without extraordinary character. This rather sweeping statement is based on an assumption that since it is God alone who makes a person an apostle, God would not trust the office of apostle to anyone who has not agreed to meet His standards of holiness and humility!

I may have used the adjective "extraordinary" to modify character, but I did not use the word "perfect." It is my strong feeling that no individual on Earth is, or will ever be, perfect in the sense of having no room for improvement in attitudes, behavior or relationships. The Greek word *teleios*, frequently translated "perfect" in the Bible, does not signify a flawless moral nature, but rather it refers to *maturity*. For example, when Jesus says, "Therefore you shall be perfect [*teleios*], just as your Father in heaven is perfect" (Matt. 5:48), He simply means that we are to live up to everything that God wants us to be. I like the way *The Message* translates this verse: "Grow up. You're kingdom subjects. Now live like it. Live out your God-created destiny. Live generously and graciously toward others, the way God lives toward you."

## Apostles Are High on the Scale

Now let's consider why the character of an apostle must be extraordinary and well above average in character.

If we agree that no one can be perfect, let's also agree on something else. Let's agree that apostles can be expected to operate further up the scale toward *teleios* than other good believers. I say this because God has a particular scale of judgment. I know this will surprise some, but consider what the Bible says in James 3:1: "My brethren, let not many of you become teachers, knowing that we shall receive a stricter judgment."

Another way of putting this is that God has one standard of judgment for leaders and another for the rest of the Body of Christ. Teachers are used as an example of leaders in James. But 1 Corinthians 12:28 says, "And God has appointed these in the church: first apostles, second prophets, third teachers." If teachers, who are number three on the list, face a strict judgment, then it follows that apostles, who are number one on the list, will face an even stricter one.

Apostles are apostles not because they are perfect, but because they have met God's standards of holiness and humility.

## Apostolic Holiness

I am aware that many believers will feel it is inappropriate to state that apostles are holy. This is probably because they have been taught that no human being can be "holy" in this life—including apostles. Martin Luther and John Calvin, the great theologians of the Reformation, taught that believers should strive for holiness and improve in holiness as time goes by, but that no one could ever say that they are holy (meaning *without sin*). This position is commonly known as "the Reformed doctrine of sanctification." It is what I was taught in seminary, and it took me quite a while to begin to see it differently.

Many churches sing the famous hymn "Holy, Holy, Holy, Lord God Almighty." This song beautifully emphasizes the holiness of God. At one point the lyrics say, "Only Thou art holy." Do you see what this implies? If the only holy being in the world is God, none of us mere human beings can be holy. The song was written from the perspective of Reformed theology.

A couple of centuries after Luther's and Calvin's time, John Wesley came along. He was influential enough to switch the paradigm from the Reformed doctrine of sanctification to what we now call "Wesleyan holiness." He dared to believe that those who serve a holy God should themselves be holy. Well-known denominations such as Methodists, Nazarenes, Salvation Army, Pentecostal Holiness, and many others follow John Wesley's teaching.

I personally believed and taught the Reformed doctrine of sanctification for many years. That is until I became deeply involved in teaching and practicing spiritual warfare in the late 1980s. It was then that I first met Cindy Jacobs who made a classic statement that I have not forgotten. She said, "When you go into spiritual warfare, you must put on the full armor of God. But if you have put on the full armor of God and if underneath you do not have a pure heart, you will have cracks in your armor!" The implication is that the devil is the first to know where those cracks are, and they can easily make you a casualty of the war!

## A Personal Paradigm Shift

This put the fear of God into me. I knew that my Reformed doctrine of sanctification would not sustain me in the intense level of intercession and spiritual warfare which God was assigning me for the decade of the 1990s. So I thoroughly examined the principles of Wesleyan holiness and concluded that it was the most biblical view of all. I could no longer be content with the notion that it didn't matter if I carried some sin in my heart as a normal part of life.

I now believe that it is possible to live without sin, one day at a time. Holiness is not merely some desirable but elusive ideal. Holiness is an attainable personal quality. The Bible says, "But as He who called you is holy, you also be holy in all your conduct" (1 Pet. 1:15). I think we can presume that God would not require us to do something that is impossible for us to do, such as being holy in all—not some, not most—of our conduct.

When I say that we can live without sin, I am not saying that anyone can ever get to the place where it is not *possible* to sin. Yes, it is possible, even probable, that each one of us will sin—most likely more than once. However, when we do sin, we confess the sin and God forgives us and cleanses us. We must never let the sun set on unconfessed sin. An occasional sin is not necessarily a character flaw. It becomes a character flaw, however, if we fail to deal with it immediately, and worse if we knowingly repeat it.

When Jesus' apostles, on two separate occasions a year and a half apart, asked Him to teach them to pray, Jesus gave them what we now know as the "Lord's Prayer." If we pray the Lord's Prayer daily, we will have what we need to keep on the track of holiness. I have been praying (not just "saying") the Lord's Prayer daily ever since I knew that I had to be holy.

## Starting the Day with No Sin

Every morning I pray, "Forgive my sins, as I forgive those who sin against me." This triggers a review of the last 24 hours to see if any sin might have arisen and gone unconfessed.

How do I really know when I have sinned? Every day I ask God to fill me with the Holy Spirit, and I can be confident that He does so, according to the promise of Luke 11:11-13. One of the benefits of having the Holy Spirit is that He convicts of sin, righteousness and judgment. If I am filled with the Holy Spirit, He will then take the responsibility of bringing those sins to mind at that time; and when He does, I confess them. This morning, for example, He did not bring anything to mind when I asked. In this way I know I can begin the day without sin in my life.

Then I pray, "Lead me not into temptation," believing that God will answer that prayer. If He does, I will not sin because I will not be tempted all day long. I plan on that. I don't expect to be tempted or to sin all day. It doesn't mean that I can't sin—and sometimes I do, but most days I don't.

To nail it down, I also pray, "Deliver me from the evil one," and if that prayer is answered as well, I will have protection throughout the day. When I go to bed at night, I can usually look back on a whole day of pleasing the Lord through living a holy life.

I expect apostles to live holy lives because personal holiness is assumed in the detailed lists of qualifications for church leadership that we have in the Bible. Take for example 1 Timothy

3:1-7, which lists the requirements for a bishop, requirements that, by extension, must apply equally (or even more) to an apostle. Few of the qualifications have to do with gifts or abilities such as leadership, casting vision, healings, prophecy, oratory or scholarship. Teaching is there, but the bulk of the qualifications have to do with character: a solid family, self-control, maturity, hospitality, moderation, peacefulness, material contentment, and qualities like those.

## Blameless with a Good Reputation

The most exacting requirements on the list are the first and the last: Being "blameless" (see 1 Tim. 3:2) and having "a good testimony among those who are outside" (1 Tim. 3:7). In order to sustain their ministry as God has designed it, apostles must be blameless. Is this possible?

Take apostle Paul for example. Let's go back to his letters to the Corinthian church. In 1 Corinthians, he roundly scolds them for divisions, for eating meat offered to idols, for taking each other to court, for tolerating immorality, for false doctrine, for getting drunk at the Lord's Supper, and on and on. He undoubtedly expected some to say, "Who does this Paul think he is? He probably does the same things and worse himself!" So in order to defuse any such reaction, Paul makes the remarkable statement in 1 Corinthians 4:4: "I know nothing against myself." Here is an apostle claiming to be blameless!

Being blameless is the only way Paul could say, later in the same chapter, "Therefore, I urge you, imitate me" (1 Cor. 4:16). This is not just some kind of odd behavior on the part of one of history's greatest apostles; this is normative for every apostle. In fact, apostles who, for any reason, cannot say to their followers, "Imitate me," would do well to reevaluate the validity of their apostolic call. It could be a symptom of a character flaw that needs to be repaired.

## Pride

One of the 1 Timothy 3 requirements for leadership is to be "not a novice, lest being puffed up with pride, he fall into the same condemnation as the devil" (1 Tim. 3:6). Pride is a surefire blockage to effective apostolic ministry. The temptation to be proud is always there because of the unusual amount of authority entrusted to apostles. One of the most frequent "canned" stereotypes that critics of the apostolic movement come up with is that apostles are arrogant, authoritarian, manipulative, self-promoting and haughty. In a word, *proud*!

Among the bona fide, God-anointed, powerful, productive, high-energy, task-oriented apostles whom I know—and those adjectives describe the great majority of them—I do not know one whom I could accuse of being proud. Superficially, I admit, some may outwardly seem to be proud in certain public settings, but rarely does that impression persist when you get to the heart level below the surface.

## Apostolic Humility

Not long ago, I found myself on the platform officially opening the annual meeting of the International Coalition of Apostles. As I recall, there were about 400 apostles present. My first remarks were, "It's wonderful to be in the same room with hundreds of humble people!" I paused to observe the reaction. Some of them showed a bit of insecurity by nervous giggling. Some looked at me skeptically as if to say, "Yeah, right!" Most smiled tolerantly to see where I was taking them.

So I explained it to them. I told them that when you think it through, no one could be a real, true, legitimate apostle who was not humble. What do I mean? I mean that we can take Jesus' axiom literally: "Whoever exalts himself will be humbled, and whoever humbles himself will be exalted" (Matt. 23:12, *NIV*). Apostles hold one of the most exalted offices in the church, according to 1 Corinthians 12:28: "*first* apostles" (emphasis added). The only way to become exalted in God's kingdom, according to Jesus, is to humble yourself. Gordon Lindsay agrees when he says, "True apostles will first manifest their apostolic ministry by humility."[4]

It would be good if we could lose some of our inhibitions against talking about humility. I know that it may be difficult to do, but I have lost mine to the extent that I have written a whole book with the title *Humility*. In it, I actually advocate that we should begin talking about our own humility a bit more than we usually have in the past. Moses did. He wrote the words, "The man Moses was very humble, more than all the men who were on the face of the earth" (Num. 12:3). Jesus did. He said, "I am humble and gentle" (Matt. 11:29, *NLT*). Paul did. He wrote, "I, Paul, myself am pleading with you by the meekness [i.e., humility] and gentleness of Christ" (2 Cor. 10:1). Notice that Paul even went so far as to equate his humility with that of Jesus!

Keep in mind that humility is a choice. Jesus said that He would exalt those who *humble themselves* (see 1 Pet. 5:6). Apostles who continue to see the blessing and anointing of God on their ministry have learned how to humble themselves. Yes, it takes time, but it gets easier with maturity. That's why the Bible warns against putting novices in leadership positions, lest they be "puffed up with pride" (see 1 Tim. 3:6).

If some apostles make the mistake of not humbling themselves, chances are that God will step in and humble them. If and when that happens, it is too late. I have already mentioned that over the time I have led the International Coalition of Apostles (ICA), I have had to dismiss some of them for serious moral failure, and force others to resign. God saw fit to humble them. They were no longer "blameless." To the extent that I have any say in the matter, I will not tolerate unbecoming conduct in an apostle. They may be restored somewhere down the road (in fact, one of them has been restored), but things will never again be the same. It is an axiom that after a Christian leader falls, he or she will never again rise up to his or her previous level of influence and authority in the Body of Christ.

Character counts! It is the *sine qua non* for qualifying and ministering as an apostle!

**Notes**

1. David Cannistraci, *Apostles and the Emerging Apostolic Movement* (Ventura, CA: Renew, 1996), p. 108.
2. Bill Hamon, *Apostles, Prophets and the Coming Moves of God* (Santa Rosa Beach, FL: Christian International, 1997), p. 39.
3. Cannistraci, *Apostles and the Emerging Apostolic Movement*, p. 107.
4. Gordon Lindsay, *Apostles, Prophets and Governments* (Dallas, TX: Christ for the Nations, Inc., 1988), p. 14.

# CHAPTER FOUR

# SPIRITUAL GIFTS AND APOSTOLIC ASSIGNMENTS

In chapter 2, I suggested that a major source of apostolic authority is the fact that God has given the spiritual gift of apostle to certain individuals of His choosing.

I feel that a book on apostling requires a serious chapter on spiritual gifts. The reason for this may be surprising to many. The majority of my ministry life has been spent in a straight-laced evangelical environment. It was only in the mid-1990s that I began moving into the charismatically inclined apostolic family of churches. One of my major disappointments when I did so was the low level of biblical understanding of spiritual gifts in most of these churches. Although I admit that I am generalizing, traditional evangelical leaders seem to have a better understanding of the biblical teaching on spiritual gifts than do the apostles and teachers of the New Apostolic Reformation.

## Charismata and Charismatics

At first glance, this will undoubtedly seem strange because the large majority of apostles would see themselves as "charismatic," which means that they base a good part of their self-identity on the fact that they move in the *charismata* (the biblical word for "spiritual gifts"). Consequently, spiritual gifts are highly important to virtually every apostle. Most of them frequently preach and teach on spiritual gifts. I suspect that it will surprise many of them, and even upset some, to read in a book like this that someone like me feels their theology of spiritual gifts might be faulty.

So, let me explain.

## George Barna's Wake-Up Call

Although I had felt for some time that the apostolic movement had a bit of room to improve in the area of spiritual gifts, I found myself keeping that issue on the back burner. It was a battle that I thought wasn't mine to fight. My wake-up call, however, came from a sociological survey on spiritual gifts released by researcher George Barna in February 2001.

Before I go on, I should explain that I have a higher than average personal interest and professional involvement in the area of spiritual gifts. I have been teaching on the subject since 1950, and I have written two books about it. In fact *Your Spiritual Gifts Can Help Your Church Grow* has become the most popular of all my books over the years, currently in its forty-sixth printing with over one-quarter of a million copies sold. Sales of the accompanying questionnaire, *Finding Your Spiritual Gifts*, have gone over one million.

I mention these credentials in order to help us understand why I was so shocked at Barna's findings. I thought that the Body of Christ was on a roll in understanding and ministering in spiritual gifts. I thought just about everybody was now catching on. I even admit that I had secretly harbored some hope that perhaps my books might have been helping. Wrong! One of George Barna's findings revealed that the number of born-again Christians who don't even believe that they have any spiritual gifts at all has actually been increasing here in America!

Barna discovered that in 1995 the percentage of born-again Christian adults who did not think they had any spiritual gift was 4 percent. Not bad. However by 2000 the percentage had risen to 21 percent! If this trend continues, it means that we could be on the threshold of a whole generation of impotent believers attending impotent churches! What potential openings for attacks from the world of darkness! Barna also discovered that many Christians don't even know what the biblical spiritual gifts really are. Some include in their lists of spiritual gifts strange things like "a sense of humor," "poetry," "a good personality," and "going to church," just to name a few![1]

It's time to sound the alarm!

## Seeking the Cause

It is one thing to know that our biblical understanding of spiritual gifts is taking a nose dive, but it is another thing to analyze this phenomenon in order to understand what might be happening behind the scenes. Others may come up with more insightful explanations, but my analysis associates this discouraging phenomenon with the apostolic movement.

The fastest growing group of churches in the U.S. during Barna's test period of 1995 to 2000 were churches of the New Apostolic Reformation. Granted, they are not the largest group, but their annual growth rate was (and still is) the highest. While these churches are almost invariably evangelistically-minded, research shows that the bulk of their growth has come from transfers from other churches, not from adult conversions to Christianity. This seems to indicate that the members of these growing apostolic churches were receiving less than ideal teaching on the subject of spiritual gifts from their previous leaders—which in itself could go a long way in explaining Barna's findings.

My hunch would be that if George Barna had asked his questions about spiritual gifts to two separate groups—namely traditional evangelicals as compared to Pentecostals, charismatics and new apostolic believers all taken together—the traditional evangelicals would have scored considerably higher in the understanding of spiritual gifts. It is true that they may not speak in tongues, prophesy, heal the sick or cast out demons as others might, but they generally have a clearer biblical understanding of how spiritual gifts are intended to operate in the Body of Christ.

Many of the transfers of church membership in the U.S. in recent years have been from the more traditional evangelical churches to the apostolic churches. My wife and I made the change in 1996. I can state with confidence that most of those who transfer membership would testify that their spiritual lives and relationship with the Lord have been kicked up a notch through their decision to change. However, I sense that their understanding of how to use spiritual gifts in the church might well have slipped, thereby contributing to Barna's findings.

## Apostolic Spiritual Genealogy

Why are many of the new apostolic churches weak on spiritual gifts? It goes back to their spiritual genealogy. New apostolic churches, for the most part, are rooted in the independent charismatic movement that began around 1970. Independent charismatic churches are generally rooted in classical Pentecostalism. Although the huge, ongoing contribution of the Pentecostal movement to the kingdom of God consists of restoring the biblical view of the person and work of the Holy Spirit, ironically two serious flaws crept into their understanding of the operation of spiritual gifts. The first flaw was that the number of spiritual gifts was only nine. The second flaw was the *situational* view of spiritual gifts as opposed to the *constitutional* view.

## "The" Nine Gifts of the Spirit

When Pentecostals in the U.S. and in other parts of the world began to be baptized or to be filled with the Holy Spirit, they started to move in some of the biblical spiritual gifts that were not being used very much in Baptist, Methodist, Presbyterian and Lutheran churches. The gifts that distinguished Pentecostals from the others, such as tongues, interpretation of tongues, prophecy, healings, discernment of spirits, and miracles, all seemed to be clustered in the first part of 1 Corinthians 12. Consequently, Pentecostal leaders, quite naturally, focused on the part of Scripture that happened to contain a list of nine spiritual gifts. In their minds, those nine gifts seemed to carry with them a qualitative distinction that set them apart from other activities found in almost all churches, Pentecostal and non-Pentecostal, such as hospitality, administration, evangelism, service, exhortation, mercy, pastoring, giving, leadership and helps.

This short list of nine gifts carried over into the charismatic movement as well. To verify this, I cite one of the nation's most highly respected charismatic theologians, J. Rodman Williams. In his textbook *Renewal Theology*, Williams dedicates 86 double-column pages to spiritual gifts. He affirms that "the gifts of the Spirit are specifically dealt with in 1 Corinthians 12:8-10"[2] and later tells the reader, "I will operate within the confines of the nine gifts."[3]

The upshot of this is that classical Pentecostals and independent charismatics typically speak of "*the* nine gifts of the Holy Spirit." Most Pentecostals would expect a sermon, book, theological essay or class on the subject of spiritual gifts to deal with only those nine gifts found in the first part of 1 Corinthians 12. At the same time, the New Testament as a whole contains a much longer list than just the nine listed in 1 Corinthians 12:8-10. Different people who specialize in spiritual gifts may reach different conclusions as to the total number of spiritual gifts, but the list I use in my two books on spiritual gifts contains 28 gifts, each with a concise, dictionary definition.[4]

The way this relates to George Barna's findings is that many members of apostolic churches have inherited the classic Pentecostal/charismatic assumption that there are only nine spiritual gifts. However, a surprisingly large number of church members, including Pentecostals, do not speak in tongues, prophesy, heal the sick, or cast out demons—even though they enjoy being around others who do! So when a researcher asks them if they have a spiritual gift, their mind tends to flash through the well-known list of nine, none of which they have (to their knowledge), and they naturally answer, "No, I don't believe I have a spiritual gift." It may just never occur to some of them that they might be ministering in one or more of the other 19 or so spiritual gifts, because in their churches those gifts are not really awarded the same status as are "the" nine. This causes them to reach the erroneous conclusion that if they don't operate in any of the nine gifts of 1 Corinthians 12:8-10, then they must not have any spiritual gift at all.

## The Situational View of Spiritual Gifts

The second common flaw in the classic Pentecostal/charismatic understanding of spiritual gifts relates to their "situational" view of the gifts. Let me explain the difference between the *situational* view of spiritual gifts and the *constitutional* view.

The situational view of spiritual gifts assumes that all of the gifts are available to be given to all believers at any time they are needed. Since an individual is filled with the Holy Spirit, all the gifts of the Holy Spirit must be resident. In other words, when a situation demands that a certain ministry be applied, God will activate in the individual the appropriate spiritual gift to accomplish that ministry. The individual might rarely, if ever, use that gift again, but it was there for the time it was needed to deal with the situation—much like an air bag in an automobile accident.

The constitutional view, however, is quite a bit different.

## The Constitutional View

The constitutional view of spiritual gifts takes more literally the biblical analogy of the Body of Christ, with gifted persons expected to function in unique capacities within the body. In the human body, for example, an eye has the attributes of vision, which is different from the attributes of a kidney or an ear or a

tongue. However, together, all the parts make up the entire body—
though eyes are always eyes, kidneys are always kidneys, and
so forth.

Likewise, in the Body of Christ, a person with the gift of
evangelist, for example, doesn't just lead one person to Christ
here and there, but ministers regularly and powerfully in leading unbelievers to Christ. The gift of evangelist, therefore,
becomes a personal attribute, a part of their *constitution*, their
"spiritual DNA," and not just a fleeting ability used in occasional situations. In this view, gifts are given as lifetime possessions,
and those who have them are responsible for using them effectively over the long haul.

The constitutional view of spiritual gifts dovetails much
more closely with the biblical idea that the collective Church
operates like a human body. It also lays the foundation for believers to focus on the gift or gifts that they have been given, developing them and improving in their use as time goes by.

The idea that I might have a gift today but not tomorrow
(the situational view) greatly reduces my incentive to spend the
time, energy and money required to develop increasing excellence in that area of ministry.

## Explaining Tongues

I believe that the situational view of spiritual gifts may have
been developed by early Pentecostal leaders to help explain
the phenomenon of tongues. All of a sudden, large numbers of
believers in Topeka or Los Angeles or other places started
speaking in tongues. As historians of the movement have doc-
umented, these early Pentecostal leaders were extremely fervent
in their spirits and in biblical power ministries, but not particularly sophisticated in their knowledge of biblical theology.
They did know, however, that tongues is one of the biblical spir-

itual gifts listed in the Bible, so they assumed that everyone who spoke in tongues must have been given the gift of tongues.

Soon afterward, they were forced to explain the subsequent phenomenon of someone who was "baptized in the Holy Spirit" but ended up speaking in tongues only once—or infrequently, at best. These people obviously did not have the ongoing gift of tongues that others apparently had, so the conclusion was that the gift had been given to them only for a certain situation (i.e., baptism in the Holy Spirit) and perhaps once in a while after that, but not as a permanent possession. This led to what I call the "situational view" of spiritual gifts. They then projected this same conclusion onto the other eight gifts.

## Roles vs. Gifts

The same phenomena of those days could just as easily (and more biblically) have been explained by the constitutional view of spiritual gifts. This simply entails keeping in mind the distinction between *spiritual gifts* and Christian *roles*.

There are certain things that every Christian is expected to do because he or she is Christian, not because he or she is gifted. For example, every Christian has a *role* of being a witness for Christ even though only a few have the gift of evangelism. Every Christian has a *role* of giving tithes and offerings, but only a few go beyond that with a gift of giving. Every Christian has a *role* of faith, but some have a spiritual gift of faith. The examples are endless. The Pentecostal view of tongues is that every believer has a *role* of speaking in tongues at least once, as the initial physical evidence of the baptism in the Holy Spirit. In my view, however, this does not necessarily have to be attributed to the spiritual *gift* of tongues.

The constitutional view of spiritual gifts has the advantage of both explaining the phenomena we see when the Holy Spirit comes in power on individuals or groups *and* remaining faithful to the biblical analogy relating spiritual gifts to the function of the parts of the human body.

## The Gift of Apostle

The spiritual gift of apostle is one of the 28 on my list of biblical spiritual gifts. It obviously would be very difficult to understand the gift of apostle through the framework of the situational view. No one would have expected Peter or Paul or John to wake up some days without the gift of apostle. Nor would they have expected the average member of the churches in Ephesus or Rome or Jerusalem to receive the gift of apostle from time to time during his or her Christian life.

Both then and now, the gift of apostle, once given by God, becomes a special attribute of the individual; and that individual is responsible for using it wisely as a good steward of the grace of God. Knowing that God has entrusted them with the gift of apostle, and not fearing that God may suddenly take that gift from them, is one thing that confers extraordinary authority on true apostles.

## Apostolic Assignments

For apostles, knowing the precise nature of their apostolic assignment raises even more their confidence in the ministry of the Holy Spirit through them.

While all apostles have the gift of apostle, not all have the same assignment. Paul writes, "Now there are diversities of gifts, but the same Spirit. There are differences of ministries, but the same Lord. And there are diversities of activities, but it is the same God who works all in all" (1 Cor. 12:4-6).

Let me explain this by using the gift of evangelist as an example. All evangelists have the gift. But some have a ministry of public evangelism, while others have the ministry of personal evangelism. Some, of course, have both. Those with a ministry of public evangelism have different activities. Some are city-wide, large campaign evangelists. Some are itinerant evangelists who travel from church to church. And others exercise their ministry of public evangelism primarily from the pulpit of the church they pastor.

I group ministries and activities under the umbrella of "assignments" or "divine assignments." God gives the gift and He also gives the assignment. The ways that different apostles minister with different assignments is one of the major features of this book. Chapters 6 and 7 will spell this out in detail, answering many questions about contemporary apostolic ministry.

**Notes**

1. Barna Research Group, Ltd., "Awareness of Spiritual Gifts Is Changing," News Release (Ventura, CA), February 5, 2001, pp. 1-2.
2. J. Rodman Williams, *Renewal Theology: Systematic Theology from a Charismatic Perspective* (Grand Rapids, MI: Zondervan Publishing House, 1996), p. 324.
3. Ibid., p. 347, footnote 1.
4. My two books on spiritual gifts are the textbook *Your Spiritual Gifts Can Help Your Church Grow* and the condensed version, *Discover Your Spiritual Gifts,* both published by Regal Books.

# CHAPTER FIVE

# THE POWER OF A TITLE

Those of us who have been reading the Bible for years are very familiar with quotes such as, "Paul, called to be an apostle of Jesus Christ through the will of God" (1 Cor. 1:1), "Paul, an apostle (not from men nor through man, but through Jesus Christ and God the Father who raised Him from the dead)" (Gal. 1:1), "Paul, an apostle of Jesus Christ by the will of God" (Col. 1:1), "Peter, an apostle of Jesus Christ" (1 Pet. 1:1), or many other similar statements. What Paul and Peter are doing is displaying their title of apostle in a public way.

## Displaying the Title

Paul specifically emphasizes his apostolic credentials in no fewer than 9 of his 13 epistles. Peter does it in both of his epistles. True, they use other titles along with "apostle." Paul calls himself a "servant" in two epistles, and Peter does the same in one of his. Paul also refers to himself as a "prisoner" in his epistle to Philemon. In the other epistles by James, John and Jude, "apostle" is not used. They choose to call themselves "servant" twice and "elder" twice.

In summary, the self identification of choice by the authors of the New Testament epistles are:

- Apostle—11 times
- Servant—5 times
- Elder—2 times
- Prisoner—1 time

There must be more significance than mere superficiality or coincidence that the title "apostle" is used more than twice as often as any other title by the leaders who wrote the New Testament epistles. One reason for this, in my opinion, is that there is power in the title. Those to whom God has given the spiritual gift of apostle and who have been entrusted with the office of apostle by human representatives of the Body of Christ, apparently are more able to function effectively in their divine assignment with the title "apostle" than they could without it.

Let's examine the origins of the title "apostle," in order to determine if it is appropriate to use today.

## Jesus Coined the Title

Where did the title "apostle" come from as applied to Christian leadership? From Jesus. He was the first to use the title in that way. After praying all night, the next morning Jesus "called His disciples to Him; and from them He chose 12 whom He also named apostles" (Luke 6:13).

The word "apostle" does not appear in the Old Testament; it is a term that Jesus specifically adapted to apply to certain leaders under the New Covenant. However, Jesus did not invent the word "apostle." It was already a common secular term in His day. The Greek word is *apóstolos*, which means "messenger" or "he that is sent" or, more specifically, "a messenger sent with a particular purpose or goal."

New Testament apostles, however, were not mere messengers in general. Peter and Paul both referred to themselves as apostles *of Jesus Christ*. This is important because such a title carries with it a dimension of great authority. It reflects an ambassadorial ranking. It is like Joe Doe, United States Ambassador to Japan. In Japan he is recognized by the title Ambassador Joe Doe or Mr. Ambassador. In order to fulfill his assignment, the title is essential because it carries the authority that has been personally delegated by the president of the United States. Without the title, Joe Doe is just Joe Doe, and high-level doors do not open to him. In this case, a title is not just optional, but it is also essential for getting the job done.

It is reasonable to conclude that Jesus had a specific purpose in choosing the title "apostle" for the 12 whom He considered special among his wider circle of disciples. That is why it seems somewhat odd that for centuries the Church has tended to steer clear of using the title. It is odd because, as I stated in chapter 2, we seem to be perfectly comfortable using titles for other governmental or foundational offices found in Ephesians 4:11. For example, for pastors we have no problem with "Pastor Mike" or "Reverend Johnson." "Evangelist Billy Graham" sounds okay. People often refer to me as "Dr. Wagner," to acknowledge that I am a teacher, and I accept that title (even though I balk at overusing it). I am secure in the fact that I have earned my Ph.D., but in personal conversation I prefer simply "Peter."

## Breaking Boundaries

"Doctor" is one thing, but how about "*Apostle* So-and-so"? I admit that it still sounds a bit strange, even to me. It breaks traditional religious boundaries. It takes us out of our comfort zones. Even so, it is part and parcel of the new paradigm that God has provided for the Church. I am thoroughly convinced that one of the things that the Spirit is saying to the churches these days is that we must get the biblical government of the church in place and that an important part of the process is to begin to use the title "apostle" when appropriate.

Is this biblical? According to the Bible it is. Actually, the New Testament uses the term "apostle" much more than it uses the other Ephesians 4:11 titles that today's church leaders seem to feel more comfortable with.

Here is the count of appearances of the words in the New Testament:

- Apostle—74
- Teacher—14

• Prophet—8
• Evangelist—3
• Pastor—3

In some circles, people prefer the title "bishop" to "apostle." This is more due to religious tradition than biblical precedent. The Catholic Church has used the title freely for centuries, and some Protestants continue to use it. The word "bishop," however, only appears four times in the New Testament as a synonym of "pastor" or "elder," but never for a senior church leader. And no one in the Bible is specifically identified as a "bishop."

Looking at those numbers, it is hard to explain why some Bible believers use "pastor" freely and disdain using "apostle," other than admitting that it is simply dictated by religious tradition. To such people I could hardly refrain from recommending my book *Freedom from the Religious Spirit.* Let's not get stuck in the past!

## The Adjective Is Not Enough

For a number of our more tentative Christian leaders, the adjective "apostolic" seems to be acceptable, while the noun "apostle" is avoided. They speak of "apostolic leadership" or "apostolic churches" or "apostolic ministry," with the implication that by doing so they are describing apostles. At times they even make the adjective a noun and refer to "the apostolic." In my opinion, this choice of words weakens the biblical church government that God desires to put into place. In fact, I looked up the word "apostolic" in the concordance and in the entire text of my *New King James Version* and I couldn't find it anywhere!

There are at least two reasons why some prefer the unbiblical adjective "apostolic" to the biblical noun "apostle." The first reason relates to people who do not believe that there are any apostles at all in the Church today, and the second relates to people who do. Let's examine both camps.

There are those who use the adjective and not the noun, in order to help argue the point that the title "apostle" was discontinued in the Church after the first 200 years or so of Church history. In chapter 1, I mentioned that the American Assemblies of God had taken this position through an official denominational "white paper." The paper attempts to argue that some people (like me!) are wrongly interpreting Scriptures such as 1 Corinthians 12:28 and Ephesians 2:20 and 4:11. It equates what I call "the problematic teaching that present-day offices of apostles and prophets should govern church ministries at all levels" with "persons with an independent spirit and an exaggerated estimate of their importance in the kingdom of God." The paper concludes by choosing to use the adjective and not the noun: "We affirm that there are and ought to be, apostolic- and prophetic-type ministries in the Church, without individuals being identified as filling such an office."[1] Now, I am not looking to engage in a war of words or doctrines, but this sounds like having your cake and eating it too! How can you have a ministry and not have the ministers minister?

It is common for those who hold this traditional position to argue that it is missionaries who are today's apostles because missionaries are sent. But this position is deceiving. For example, in Luke 10, Jesus sent out 70 to preach the Gospel of the kingdom. All 70 were sent as messengers (*apóstolos*, Greek for "messenger" or "he that is sent"), but only 12 of them were actually apostles.

The biblical principle is this: All apostles are sent, but not all those who are sent are apostles.

## An Entry-Level Approach

On the other hand, some who *do* believe that we have apostles in churches today still prefer to use "apostolic" instead of "apostle" because they feel that the adjective is less threatening and therefore provides a more entry-level approach to those who might be seeking. I will admit that this is commendable, and there might be some wisdom in doing so—at least for a limited time.

An example of this is the first widely circulated book on the apostolic movement published in Australia, *The 21ˢᵗ Century Church Out There*, edited by Ben Gray. In that book, only the adjective "apostolic" is used. However, the second Australian book, *The Apostolic Revolution* by David Cartledge, overcomes the reluctance of the Ben Gray book and uses the noun "apostle" freely. This, along with many other factors, including key apostolic conferences convened by Ben Gray, have brought Australia to the place of being possibly the most advanced nation *as a nation* in understanding and applying apostolic government to church life.

I think that John Eckhardt, in his book *Leadershift*, makes a very good point. He is a strong advocate of using the title "Apostle" and for years has cordially accepted the designation Apostle John Eckhardt. In fact he has it on his church marquee in inner city Chicago. In his book he argues that when the government of the church is in place under one or more apostles, then every church can be an apostolic church, every believer should be an apostolic believer, every teacher should be an apostolic teacher, every evangelist should be an apostolic evangelist, every pastor should be an apostolic pastor, and so on. If this is the case, then it is clear that the adjective "apostolic" has its place, but not as a substitute for "apostle" as a noun.

## Is "Apostle" a Red Flag?

The propriety of using the title "apostle" is being vigorously discussed wherever church leaders desire to move a bit closer to the cutting edge. I'm not going to mention names, but I was interested in reading a dialogue on the Internet recently that went something like this:

Person A: "A pastoral vision fails to provide a large enough foundation for the church. It wants to take care of the sheep whom we have. An evangelistic vision focuses outward primarily, which is important. However it can fail to nurture the sheep. It is necessary to have an apostolic vision of the kingdom of God in place in order to support the superstructure God wants to build."

Person B: "I agree whole-heartedly. However, I've shied away from using the title and have sought to focus more on the function—mostly because the language means so many things to so many different people."

Person A: "Some people put themselves forward as 'apostles' when they aren't really apostles. Others function as apostles, but have no desire for the title. It is a 'red flag' term for so many people."

These two individuals are agreeing that a danger of using the title "apostle" is that some might take offense, that it might precipitate disunity in the Body of Christ. I think they are making an accurate observation, but I also think that their fears are not altogether justified. I am concerned that some will be so consumed with preserving the status quo that Christian unity based on political correctness and adhering to the least common denominator actually becomes an end in itself. When this happens, it is very difficult to make positive changes and advance the kingdom of God, especially when God is trying to form a new wineskin. Moreover, this approach is simply based more in fear than in sound theology. Fear of stirring things up. Fear of rejection. Fear of argument. Fear of accusation.

However, having said that, I must also say that I have found much less opposition to accepting the gift and office of apostle than I had originally expected. We went public with the idea of the New Apostolic Reformation with the National Symposium on the Postdenominational Church, held at Fuller Seminary in 1996. To my knowledge, no broad-scale wave of opposition has materialized since that symposium. Consequently, the risk that the title of apostle could be a "red flag" that might set the movement back may not be as much of a threat as some imagine.

## Apostles Are Not Made Overnight

One of the most insightful books on apostolic leadership is *Apostles* by Bill Scheidler. Two of his chapters contain a personal interview with Dick Iverson, founder of one of America's foremost apostolic networks, Ministers Fellowship International, out of Portland, Oregon. Dick Iverson is one who has functioned for years as an apostle, but who, until recently, resisted accepting the title. One reason for this was that he had seen the term abused so much in the past. Some people were even suspected of calling themselves apostles for their own material enrichment. Unwise prophets would at times aid and abet this by off-the-cuff prophecies that a certain person was an apostle.

Iverson tells this story: "I had a young man in his twenties in my office this morning. He said that he was an apostle, and that when he goes back to his homeland, he expects they will receive him as an apostle. Well, that may happen in twenty years from now. But for him to go back and somehow expect to be a recognized apostle overnight—I personally don't think that will happen."[2]

## How a Person Is Recognized as an Apostle

There is no single accepted process for formally recognizing and pronouncing that a person is an apostle. However, in order to agree that someone like the young man in Dick Iverson's office is really an apostle, it would have to be affirmed in each of four ways: (1) The apostle needs to know God's call personally; (2) The leadership of his own local church needs to affirm it; (3) The congregation of the apostle's local church needs to agree, and (4) Those whom the apostle has established and grounded in the faith will recognize him.[3]

## Struggling with the Title

I like the way that Apostle Trevor Newport of England describes his experience of coming to terms with being an apostle.[4] Newport, a member of the International Coalition of Apostles, had been a pastor for 14 years before he began to hear the Lord say, "I have made you an apostle—please accept it." This was difficult because he had already decided never to call himself an apostle. He struggled with the issue for three years.

A breaking point came when he sat under Colin Urquhart, another well-known British apostle. At a pastors' conference, Urquhart said, "I have been struggling for three years with accepting the apostolic call." That got Trevor's attention. After the conference, Trevor Newport prayed and simply said, "Okay, Lord, I accept the apostolic call, whatever it means."

## The Power of a Title

"Two weeks later," Newport says, "I was in a prayer meeting with about 8 others when, all of a sudden, the presence of God filled the room. We were all affected by it and could not move or speak. All I could move were my eyes! Then I saw three angels come down from heaven with Jesus in the midst. The three angels stayed outside of the door of our prayer room and Jesus came in on His own. He came straight up to me and said these words: 'Hi, Trev, it's your brother Jesus here. I've come to tell you that your ministry is just about to start. 'Bye!' I then saw Him join the three angels and go back to heaven. It was awesome! I did not realize what was happening or the effect that it would have on my ministry.

"Up until that time I only had one church that was still in its pioneer stage. Then, from that visitation on, pastors kept calling me and asking me if they could come under my covering. I had not announced anything to anyone about that!

"Within two years, Life Changing Ministries had grown to 8 churches in the UK, 17 churches in Sri Lanka, 25 churches in Nepal, 1 church in Japan, many churches in India, and 1 church in Colorado. I have now ministered in 50 countries and written 16 books."

## Three Years

When I found that both Trevor Newport and Colin Urquhart had struggled for three years to accept the title of apostle once they began to hear God about it, I retraced my own experience and found that, surprisingly enough, my process took three years as well. The first prophetic word I received that I had the anointing of an apostle came through Cindy Jacobs in July 1995, and the second through an intercessor, Margaret Moberly, two months later. I had no idea as to what I should do about it at that time. Early in 1998 God spoke to me again, this time in a public meeting through Prophet Jim Stevens. I then had no doubt that I would have to go public, but still I was not yet ready.

My hesitation came from the fact that I didn't know what kind of an apostle I was. It was only later that year that I began to understand different kinds of apostolic spheres. Once I could define my sphere of authority, I was ready to accept the title and receive the divine power that accompanied it. I knew that I wasn't a vertical apostle like most of my apostolic friends. Clarity and freedom came as soon as I captured the concept of horizontal apostles. When I knew that I was a horizontal apostle, I was ready to accept the title.

**Notes**

1. "Endtime Revival—Spirit-Led and Spirit Controlled: A Response Paper to Resolution 16," subsection "Deviant Teachings Disapproved," issued by the General Presbytery of the General Council of the Assemblies of God, August 11, 2000.
2. Bill Scheidler, *Apostles: The Fathering Servant* (Portland, OR: CityBible Publishing, 2001), p. 191.
3. Ibid., pp. 181-182.
4. This account is excerpted from personal correspondence from Trevor Newport to the author, January 26, 2001.

# CHAPTER SIX

# APOSTOLIC SPHERES

Throughout this book I have reiterated that the major characteristic that distinguishes apostles from other members of the Body of Christ is their extraordinary God-given authority. The New Apostolic Reformation is the most radical change in the way of doing church since the Protestant Reformation, and of all the different changes that could be listed, number one is *the amount of spiritual authority delegated by the Holy Spirit to individuals.*

## Biblical Examples

Let's look at some biblical examples of what it means for an apostle to exercise authority:

- *Apostle Peter:* "There were also false prophets among the people, even as there will be false teachers among you, who will secretly bring in destructive heresies, even denying the Lord who bought them, and bring on themselves swift destruction" (2 Pet. 2:1). This is strong language! There is no wavering here, nor any hints of insecurity.

- *Apostle James:* "Therefore I judge that we should not trouble those from among the Gentiles who are turning to God" (Acts 15:19). This has gone down in history as one of the most decisive apostolic declarations ever made. (I will come back to James and the authority he displayed at the Council of Jerusalem later.)

- *Apostle John:* "If anyone comes to you and does not bring this doctrine, do not receive him into your house nor greet him; for he who greets him shares in his evil deeds" (2 John 10). John is very sure of himself and of his teaching! His authority is nothing that he denies or hides. He is very clear that what he says better not be contradicted.

• *Apostle Paul:* "O foolish Galatians! Who has bewitched you that you should not obey the truth . . . Are you so foolish? Having begun in the Spirit, are you now being made perfect by the flesh?" (Gal. 3:1,3). Paul has few inhibitions when he severely reprimands certain fellow believers.

In another place, Paul sounded quite a bit like apostle John in the quote from above: "And if anyone does not obey our word in this epistle, note that person and do not keep company with him, that he may be ashamed" (2 Thess. 3:14). Apparently anyone who disagreed with Paul was in serious trouble!

## Apostolic Spheres Determine Apostolic Authority

Read through the book of Acts and the epistles and you will see many similar quotes from the apostles. There is little room to question that biblical apostles possessed extraordinary authority. But let's go one step further. Exactly where did their apostolic authority function? It did not function everywhere; it only functioned within the *apostolic sphere(s)* of each individual apostle.

Take for example Paul's relationship with the believers in the city of Corinth. It is a good case in point because in the church at Corinth there happened to be some outspoken believers who actually questioned Paul's apostolic authority. They had decided that they were not going to submit to him. Big mistake! Paul wrote 2 Corinthians 10 and 11 in order to address them directly and set them straight.

## Paul's Critics

What were those critics saying about Paul? They made four charges:

1. *Paul was ugly and boring!* "'For his letters,' they say, 'are weighty and powerful, but his bodily presence is weak, and his speech contemptible.'" (2 Cor. 10:10).

2. *Paul was not as good as the original 12 apostles!* In response, Paul had to affirm: "For I consider that I am not at all inferior to the most eminent apostles" (2 Cor. 11:5).

3. *Paul was money hungry!* "Did I commit sin in abasing myself that you might be exalted, because I preached the gospel of God to you free of charge? I robbed other churches, taking wages from them to minister to you. And when I was present with you, and in need, I was a burden to no one, for what was lacking the brethren who came from Macedonia supplied. And in everything I kept myself from being burdensome to you, and so I will keep myself" (2 Cor. 11:7-9).

4. *Paul was a self-appointed apostle, and therefore he had no authority!* "For even if I should boast somewhat about our authority, which the Lord gave us for edification and not for your destruction, I shall not be ashamed" (2 Cor. 10:8).

## Boasting About Authority

Paul, not surprisingly, was considerably upset by these accusations. He addressed them directly and firmly. But he also addressed them more broadly by explaining the concept of apostolic spheres. Paul not only knew that he had extraordinary authority, but he also went so far as to "boast" about it several times, in 2 Corinthians 10 and 11.

The Greek word for "boasting" means to glory in the acts of God. In 2 Corinthians 10:8, Paul says that he "boasts" about his authority, quickly adding that his authority comes directly from God. Therefore, Paul was not exalting himself when he boasted, he was exalting God, who had chosen to give him divine *exousía*, or "authority."

Paul was acutely aware that the apostolic authority given to him by God could only be exercised in certain places at certain times. He was not an apostle to the whole Body of Christ everywhere. He wrote to the Corinthians, "Am I not an apostle? Am I not free? Have I not seen Jesus Christ our Lord? Are you not my work in the Lord? *If I am not an apostle to others,* yet doubtless I am to you" (1 Cor. 9:1-2). I italicized that phrase because in it Paul openly admits that he is not an apostle to everybody. For example, he was not an apostle in Alexandria or in Jerusalem or in Rome. But he definitely *was* an apostle in Corinth as well as in Ephesus, Philippi, Galatia, and many other places included in his apostolic spheres.

## Boasting Within Spheres

Paul applied his boasting about his divine authority to specific spheres in 2 Corinthians 10 and 11. Below are two quotes from these chapters in which I italicize the appearances of the words "boast" and "sphere":

"We, however, will not *boast* beyond measure, but within the limits of the *sphere* which God appointed us—a *sphere* which especially includes you. [In other words, the Corinthians are under Paul's apostolic authority because they are included in his

God-given sphere.] For we are not extending ourselves beyond our *sphere*, for it was to you that we came with the gospel of Christ; not *boasting* of things beyond measure, that is, in other men's labors, but having hope, that as your faith is increased, we shall be greatly enlarged by you in our *sphere*" (2 Cor. 10:13-15).

"As the truth of Christ is in me, no one shall stop me from this *boasting* in the regions of Achaia" (2 Cor. 11:10). Achaia was the Roman province that included Corinth, clearly one of Paul's assigned spheres. He obviously would not have said this about India where Thomas had gone.

## Limits of Apostolic Authority

Let me summarize this with what I believe is one of the more important thoughts of this book: *Apostles have awesome, divinely imparted authority, but outside their God-determined sphere they don't have any more authority than any other member of the Body of Christ!*

This is important because many leaders in today's apostolic movement could stand to improve their practical understanding of the general principle of apostolic spheres as well as their knowledge of what these spheres are and how they can be defined. As a result of this dearth of knowledge, some apostolic ministry not only tends to be misunderstood, but it also can actually be rejected by those who have experienced attempts to apply it in the wrong spheres. Unfortunately, some apostles think they carry the same apostolic authority wherever they go. This is dangerous because the damage they do when they are outside of their spheres can cause permanent harm to the Church.

As I detailed in chapter 4, all apostles, by definition, have the spiritual gift of apostle. However not all apostles have the same ministry or activity. This statement is an application of 1 Corinthians 12:4-6: "Now there are diversities of gifts, but the same Spirit. There are differences of ministries but the same

Lord. And there are diversities of activities, but it is the same God who works all in all."

## Apostolic Ministries and Activities

All apostles obviously have been given the gift of apostle. What, then, are some of their different ministries and activities? As I attempt to answer this question, I want to make it clear that my research methodology is not philosophical or theological (in the classical sense) nor exegetical or revelational, but rather phenomenological. I am not saying that any of these methodologies is right or wrong. Phenomenology clearly is not superior to exegesis. It is merely my personal choice.

The phenomenological approach leads me to employ terms not found in the Bible, because I believe it is not necessary to only use the *Word* of God but to also combine the Word of God with accurate observations of the present-day *works* of God. I am not approaching this so much from the question of what God *ought* to do as much as what God *is actually doing*. What the Spirit *has said* to the churches is one thing, but what the Spirit is *now saying* to the churches is another.

Let's look at the three broadest categories of apostolic ministry that have become clear at the present time. I say "present time" because further research may turn up more categories or might demand refinement of these. My names for these three categories of apostolic ministry are "vertical apostles," "horizontal apostles" and "workplace apostles."

## Vertical Apostles

Most apostles are vertical apostles. They lead networks of churches or ministries or individuals who look to the apostle for spiritual "covering," they are comfortable under the authority of that particular apostle, and they are accountable to him or her. A biblical prototype of a vertical apostle is the apostle Paul. Many churches looked to Paul for their apostolic accountability, as did individuals such as Timothy and Titus. Paul's relationship to Titus is very instructive on this topic.

Parenthetically, the labeling of the epistles to Timothy and Titus as the "Pastoral Epistles" was done from the traditional non-apostolic paradigm. However, they are not Pastoral Epistles; they are clearly "Apostolic Epistles." Timothy and Titus were not local church pastors; they were vertical apostles, members of Paul's apostolic team. To my knowledge, the first biblical commentary that treats these epistles as apostolic rather than pastoral is *Obtainable Destiny* by Steve Hickey.

In writing to Titus, for example, Paul says, "For this reason I left you in Crete, that you should set in order the things that are lacking" (Titus 1:5). One of the major job descriptions of all apostles is to "set things in order." Then Paul goes on, "and appoint elders in every city as I commanded you" (Titus 1:5). Back in those days the "elders" were those who functioned as pastors of the churches (all of which, by the way, were house churches). Thus, Titus was the vertical apostle who was overseeing the pastors and churches in Crete.

When I compiled my first book on the subject of apostolic ministry, *The New Apostolic Churches*, I invited 18 apostles to write first-person accounts of the initiation and operation of their own apostolic networks. They were all vertical apostles. They were "vertical" in the sense that each of them had a network to which they provided apostolic oversight. For each of them, the primary apostolic sphere in which their authority enjoyed a divine anointing that was also recognized by their followers was their network. Vertical apostles are so common that, back in those days, the mid-1990s, it had never even occurred to me that there might be other kinds of apostles.

## Horizontal Apostles

When I said earlier that it took me three years from the time I knew that I was an apostle until I would accept the title of apostle, the major obstacle for me was that I didn't know what kind of apostle I was. All of the apostles I had come into contact with were vertical apostles, and I knew I was not one of them. The breakthrough came when Roger Mitchell, a friend of mine from England, suggested to me that there might be both vertical and horizontal apostles. I immediately knew that I fit the category of horizontal apostle, and I was then ready to step up to the plate with the assignment that God had given me.

Horizontal apostles, unlike vertical apostles, do not have churches or ministries or individuals under them for whom they furnish primary spiritual accountability. Rather, they serve peer-level leaders in helping them to connect with each other for different purposes. Our best biblical example is James of Jerusalem who convened the Council of Jerusalem in order to deal with the issue of whether Gentiles needed to be circumcised and become "Jews" in order to be saved.

It is good to keep in mind that this James was not one of the original 12 apostles. There were two apostles named James among the original 12. One we know very little about, and the other was a son of Zebedee and a member of Jesus' inner circle of Peter, James and John. That James was killed by Herod in Acts 12. This James of Jerusalem was a blood brother of Jesus, a son of Mary and Joseph. He was the leader in the church of Jerusalem.

I mention this because the apostles who came to Jerusalem at James's invitation were vertical apostles, such as Peter, John, Paul, Matthew, Apollo, Barnabas, Thomas, and the rest. That was an apostolic dream team! I have a strong suspicion that none of those vertical apostles could have successfully called the Jerusalem Council; only James could.

Vertical apostles are not ordinarily inclined to seek each other out and spend time with each other, especially if they're exceedingly busy (as most apostles are) or if they don't feel a great affinity for one another. Think, for example, of Peter and Paul. Clearly, they were not the best of friends. They seemed to dislike each other to the point that each criticized the other in the Bible. Paul rebuked Peter to his face because he wouldn't eat with Gentiles (see Gal. 2:11-12). Peter wrote that Paul's epistles were hard to understand and dangerous (see 2 Pet. 3:16). My point is that if either Paul or Peter had called the Jerusalem Council, the other probably wouldn't have shown up. But James, a horizontal apostle, convened it and they both went.

## Issuing an Apostolic Declaration

James had full apostolic authority at the Jerusalem Council. I enjoy this story because I can identify with the situation on a personal level. On many occasions, I have done exactly what James did. First of all, James allowed every apostle present the opportunity to say what they felt about the issue at hand. We know that James did this because Acts 15:13 says, "And after they had become silent." The Bible doesn't tell us how long the meetings lasted. I suspect they lasted a long time because I have yet to find an apostle who is at a loss for words.

Notice how James proceeded. He did not take a vote or form a commission to study the matter further or convene an executive council—as many ecclesiastical bodies do today. James said simply, "Men and brethren, listen to me" (Acts 15:13). Here is an apostle at his best. After listening to the other apostles, James didn't just have an opinion, he had the mind of the Lord. And because the whole meeting was enveloped with a Spirit-directed apostolic atmosphere, what did all these big-time apostles do? They listened to James!

The upshot was that James issued an apostolic declaration that turned out to be the most important missiological statement this side of the cross. James said, "Therefore, I judge that we should not trouble those from among the Gentiles who are turning to God" (Acts 15:19). Notice the use of the first person singular in his statement: "*I* judge." This is an apostle doing what an apostle is supposed to do: hearing what the Spirit is saying to the churches.

Whereas every believer can and should hear directly from the Holy Spirit, it is only the apostles, in proper relation to prophets, who hear what the Spirit is saying to the churches. Parents hear what the Spirit is saying to their families. CEOs hear what the Spirit is saying to their businesses. Teachers hear what the Spirit is saying to their classes. Pastors hear what the Spirit is saying to their church (singular). But apostles, along with prophets, are those who hear what the Spirit is saying to the churches (plural). That is what Paul means when he writes, "[The mystery of Christ] which in other ages was not made known to the sons of men, as it has now been revealed by the Spirit to His holy *apostles* and *prophets*" (Eph. 3:5, emphasis added).

Notice also the response of the apostles who were present. They gladly received the authoritative word from James. "It pleased the apostles and the elders and the whole church" (Acts 15:22). "It seemed good to the Holy Spirit and us" (Acts 15:28). James had unbelievable authority because he was functioning in his God-given sphere as a horizontal apostle.

However, when the apostles moved on from the Council of Jerusalem, they were no longer under James's authority. His authority as a horizontal apostle for this particular matter began when he convened the Council and ended when he dismissed it.

## The Power of Apostolic Decrees

We are accustomed to seeing supernatural power released through intercessory prayer, but it is a new thought for many of us that similar power can be released by an apostolic decree. The fact is, God does certain things in response to a declaration such as the one James proclaimed in the Council of Jerusalem that otherwise (as far as we know) He might not have done.

The two forms of tapping into divine authority are described in Job 22. The petition form is in verse 27: "You will make your *prayer* to Him, He will hear you, and you will pay your vows" (emphasis added). The proclamation form is in verse 28: "You will also *declare* a thing, and it will be established for you; so light will shine on your ways" (emphasis added).

A case in point is Moses on the banks of the Red Sea. "And the Lord said to Moses, 'Why do you cry to me? Tell the children of Israel to go forward. But lift up your rod and stretch out your hand over the sea and divide it. And the children of Israel shall go on dry ground through the midst of the sea'" (Exod. 14:15-16). God told Moses specifically that intercession "crying to me" would not do it in this case; an apostolic decree was necessary. We must know when it is time to move from petition to proclamation. It takes courage to do this.

Back in 2001 I had become aware of the importance of moving from petition to proclamation, but I had never put the theory into practice. By then I knew that I was an apostle, but I was not yet comfortable in making a public apostolic decree, much less expecting it to carry with it the spiritual authority that would actually cause something to happen. This changed when I was leading a huge international prayer conference in Hannover, Germany, in October 2001.

## Mad Cow Disease

This may sound trivial, but the principle is powerful. My wife, Doris, and I are beefsteak eaters. One of our customary family splurges is that when we travel, we try to eat at the finest prime steak houses. We did this in Hanover, but I began to notice that the menus all said "Argentine beef" or "American beef." It suddenly dawned on me that the reason the German steakhouses couldn't serve German beef was because of a devastating epidemic of mad cow disease! Since Doris and I are farmers, we became incensed that innocent German farmers could be victimized by this plague.

I hadn't given too much thought to it, however, until I was sitting in a meeting in which the power of God had fallen. I was startled when the word of God came to me: "Take authority over mad cow disease!" Such a thing had never occurred to me, so I began to process and pray over it. Since I was in charge, I needed to ask no one's permission. By the time I got to the platform I could sense a strong divine anointing. When I began to describe the situation to the 2,500 delegates from over 60 nations, I broke down into an embarrassing fit of weeping and sobbing. I then took my apostolic authority and decreed that mad cow disease would come to an end in Europe and the UK. The whole assembly noisily agreed with me and encouraged me.

That was October 1, 2001. A month later a friend of mine sent me a newspaper article from England saying that the epidemic had broken and that the last reported case of mad cow disease had been on September 30, 2001, the day before the apostolic decree! By sharing this, I am not implying that I have any inherent supernatural power. I am implying that when apostles hear the word of God clearly and when they decree His will, history can change like it did with James of Jerusalem.

## Workplace Apostles

A third significant broad sphere of apostolic ministry is workplace apostles (sometimes referred to as "kings"). The vertical and horizontal apostles conduct their ministry primarily in what could be called the "nuclear church." Workplace apostles conduct their ministry primarily in the "extended church." Just as sociologists distinguish between the nuclear family and the extended family, I believe that we can do the same with the church.

The concept of apostles in the workplace is such a new and rapidly developing area of understanding that, instead of expanding on it here, I have chosen to develop it in an entire chapter later on.

## Spheres Are Crucial

Apostles can never become everything that God wants them to be unless they are fully conscious of the sphere(s) of ministry to which God has assigned each of them. A good beginning point for understanding apostolic spheres is distinguishing between vertical apostles, horizontal apostles and workplace apostles.

And then there are several other subcategories of spheres (particularly for those who are leaders) that give further direction in knowing how we all fit together into the Body of Christ. We will examine some of these in the next chapter.

# CHAPTER SEVEN

# WHERE DO WE ALL FIT?

In the previous chapter I introduced the terms "vertical apostle," "horizontal apostle" and "workplace apostle." I am now going to suggest several additional terms that might also be applied to different types of apostles. Some readers may think I am overcomplicating things. While I understand that might well appear to be the case, my intention is just the opposite. I am attempting to *simplify* things—at least for those of us who are specialists—and to try and answer the question, Where do we all fit into God's plan for apostleship?

## Specialists Need Detail

This chapter may actually be more suited to those who desire to be specialists in the area of apostolic ministry than to believers in general. It brings to mind certain taxonomies of livestock as an illustration of the some of the benefits that a richness of detail can provide.

Doris and I are dairy farmers. As such, one of our areas of expertise is dairy cattle. Doris was a member of the New York State 4-H dairy cattle judging team. I have my undergraduate degree in dairy production, and I was on the Rutgers University dairy cattle judging team. Thus, we both probably qualify as specialists in that relatively small area of interest.

When Doris and I are driving down the highway and we see animals in a field, we do not react the way probably the majority of other motorists react. Most people would exclaim, "Look at the cows!" They thereby display their ability to tell cows from horses or sheep—which is admittedly all that most people need! A few of them might also observe that they are dairy cattle rather than beef cattle. If we saw them, however, we would invariably say, "Look at the Holsteins!" Unlike nonspecialists, it is very important to Doris and me to know that at that moment we are not looking at Guernseys or Ayrshires or Jerseys or Brown Swiss.

Applying this to apostolic ministry, much of the Christian public would admittedly do well just to be able to tell the difference between apostles and prophets. That is as far as they probably need to go. However, leaders who are closely involved with apostles, apostolic churches, apostolic ministries or apostolic teaching will be grateful for this apostolic taxonomy.

## Apostles Are Servants

In chapter 1, I mentioned that a pioneer movement of apostles sprang up after World War II, but some mistakes were made and many of those movements turned out to be relatively short-lived. One of the mistakes of some apostles was to allow themselves to become overly authoritarian. My friend Leo Lawson likes to contrast what he calls "World War II apostles" with the "Microsoft apostles"—who are more characteristic of today's New Apostolic Reformation. Microsoft apostles strive to be much more relational than dictatorial. This allows them to function more as servants than otherwise might be possible.

But can apostles really be servants? The question is not surprising. After all, in the Bible apostles are labeled with glowing terms such as "first" (see 1 Cor. 12:28) and "foundation" (see Eph. 2:20). Among all of the disciples that Jesus had, the 12 apostles constituted the most elite group. I have described in detail the unbelievable authority that characterizes apostles. How could someone as exalted as an apostle turn out to be a genuine servant as well? I would answer that question with the bold suggestion that no one can actually be a true apostle *at all* unless they are also a servant!

## Apostolic Leadership and Servanthood

Two of Jesus' apostles, James and John, could answer that question by firsthand experience. At one point they wanted to exalt themselves. They wanted to be Jesus' chief lieutenants in the Kingdom! Jesus rebuked them for this and used the opportunity to teach them and the other apostles a profound lesson on servant leadership. He first told them that apostles must not be like Gentiles and "lord it over [other people]" (Mark 10:42). Jesus then went to the positive side and said, "Whoever desires to become great among you shall be your servant" (v. 43). Thus, according to Jesus Himself, apostolic leadership (as contrasted to secular leadership) is based on servanthood. There is no other way to attain it.

Notice that Jesus does not say there is anything wrong with wanting to become great. However, He does say that in the kingdom of God, apostolic leadership does not come through coercion or self-imposition. It cannot be demanded. It cannot be claimed. It must be earned. If the litmus test of an apostle is that he or she has followers, then those followers must perceive the apostle to be their servant before they will decide to follow.

Keep in mind that the only opinion that really counts as to whether a given apostle is a servant or not is the opinion of the apostle's followers. Individuals in other apostolic spheres may get on a certain apostle's case and question whether he or she is behaving like a servant, but their opinion has little weight as long as those in the apostle's own sphere do perceive him or her to be their servant. Servanthood consists of the fact that the followers believe the decisions the apostle makes are ultimately for their benefit. Because of that, they accept their apostle's decisions and they gladly stick with the apostle.

## Foundational vs. Reformational Apostles

Roger Mitchell once suggested to me that most apostles will fit into one of two categories of primary apostolic characteristics: "foundational apostles" or "reformational apostles."

Foundational apostles are those who move out to take new territory. They are boundary breakers. They color outside of the lines. Paul would have been a foundational apostle. He said, "I have made it my aim to preach the gospel, not where Christ was named, lest I should build on another man's foundation" (Rom. 15:20). Paul planted the church in Corinth and later wrote back to the believers there, "As a wise master builder I have laid the foundation, and another builds on it" (1 Cor. 3:10). Well-known foundational apostles from history would include men such as Patrick of Ireland, William Carey, Hudson Taylor, and many others.

Reformational apostles, on the other hand, move in to regain territory once claimed by foundational apostles but that was mostly or partially lost over time due to negative spiritual forces. John, who took over the church in Ephesus, which Paul had planted, might serve as a biblical example. Others who have made a mark on Christian history would include men such as Martin Luther, John Wesley and Jonathan Edwards, to name a few.

I would see myself more as a foundational apostle than a reformational apostle. I enjoy breaking new ground, but my attention span for building on the foundation I have laid is relatively short.

## Eight Apostolic Activities

"Foundational" and "reformational" are generalized terms. Now, let's be much more specific. I am going to list four subcategories of vertical apostles and four of horizontal apostles. Both foundational apostles and reformational apostles can be located in each of these eight kinds of apostolic activity. I call these "activities" in reference to 1 Corinthians 12:4-6, where it speaks of "gifts," "ministries" and "activities." Under the "gift" of apostle (which all apostles have), some apostles have different "ministries," including vertical, horizontal and workplace; while some vertical and horizontal apostles engage in different "activities" embracing these eight subcategories.

Recognizing these eight apostolic activities could go a long way in preventing the frustration of what can be called "pseudo authority." It will help apostles more clearly recognize the exact sphere(s) to which God has assigned them and within which He has delegated to them true apostolic authority. Hopefully, it will also help prevent apostles from attempting to exercise authority outside of their sphere(s). Trouble is brewing when one apostle steps into another apostle's sphere and begins to take over! This ends up in a hurtful exhibition of pseudo authority. Recognizing where one sphere of authority ends and another begins should help keep such a thing from happening.

## Four Activities of Vertical Apostles

The chief distinguishing characteristic of vertical apostles is that they are at the head of an ongoing organization of some type. They are at the top, but not because they have successfully climbed the corporate ladder or some other hierarchy. They are at the top because the relationships they have built with the others have awarded them the leadership role. They have proven themselves as servants. They serve the others by leading them. They exercise their apostolic authority for the benefit of their followers.

Vertical apostles provide a 24/7 spiritual "covering" for others in their network. They consider themselves successful if they are somehow able to help those who follow them become everything that God wants them to be.

There are four subcategories, or activities, of vertical apostles.

### Ecclesiastical Apostles
Based on my observations, I would estimate that ecclesiastical apostles constitute the largest number of all the categories of

apostolic activities. This is where apostle Paul would have fit. Ecclesiastical apostles are given a sphere that includes a number of churches, with some expanding to include certain parachurch ministries as well.

The pastors of the churches and leaders of parachurch ministries within the network look to the apostle for their spiritual accountability. The term "apostolic network" generally refers to an ecclesiastical network. Whereas denominations were once upon a time the new wineskins into which God was pouring new wine, apostolic networks now appear to be the new wineskins of the Second Apostolic Age.

Frequently, pastors receive their ordination to ministry at the hands of the apostle. The apostle is their protection, their spiritual father or mother. Ecclesiastical apostles have permission to speak into the lives of the pastors they serve, both for encouragement and for rebuke when necessary. This covenant relationship is sealed and perpetuated by the pastors giving a tithe of their personal income to the apostle. If it is not a tithe per se, usually there is some other kind of ongoing financial support of the apostle. The followers trust the discretion of the apostles to use the money wisely both to meet their own personal needs and to advance the kingdom of God.

Some better-known examples of ecclesiastical apostles today would include Ché Ahn of Harvest International Ministries, based in Pasadena, California (5,000 churches in 41 nations); Larry Kreider of DOVE Christian Fellowship International, based in Ephrata, Pennsylvania (98 churches in 9 nations); Bill Hamon of Christian International, based in Santa Rosa Beach, Florida (405 churches and 605 ministries in 16 nations); Naomi Dowdy of Global Leadership Network, based in Singapore (490 churches in 17 nations); and Enoch Adeboye, based in Nigeria (6,000 churches in 50 nations)—and there are thousands of others like them.

### Apostolic Team Members

Most apostles develop a leadership team of one kind or another to support them in their apostolic ministry. Members of the team frequently include spouses, prophets, administrators, close friends, financial supporters, and others. Generally speaking, however, one apostle heads the network. A few, on the other hand, choose to bring other peer-level apostles onto their leadership team. This requires a special kind of "Microsoft apostle," but when it can be properly done, it greatly expands the possibility of including more churches in the network.

In my book *Churchquake!*, I go into considerable detail explaining why there is a numerical limit to the number of churches that can participate in a healthy ecclesiastical apostolic network.[1] This is based on the axiom that apostolic networks (as contrasted to denominations) are held together by personal relationships instead of by legal, bureaucratic, organizational structures. It is essential, therefore, that the leader of the network (the apostle) maintain personal relationships with the pastors of all the churches of the network. Depending on a certain set of variables, the range of churches in which this can happen is somewhere between 50 and 150 churches.

This range would apply to networks under one apostle. But if networks are headed by an apostolic team, then the more apostles on the team, the more churches can be brought into this relational structure. The members of the apostolic team may not be the head apostle of the network as a whole, but as apostolic team members, they minister much in the same way, under the ecclesiastical apostle.

### Functional Apostles

Functional apostles do not oversee or provide apostolic covering to a number of churches. Rather, they have been given apostolic authority over individuals or groups who operate within a certain type of specialized ministry. Their followers may be under a personal covering of another leader. For example, they might be members of a local church and, as such, accountable to their pastor. Still, in a particular area of ministry or with a particular affinity group, their followers might also look to a functional apostle for direction, discipling and accountability for excellence in that area.

Jane Hansen of Aglow International would be an example. She is a recognized apostle and a member of the International Coalition of Apostles (ICA). She is also a member of a local church and accountable to her pastor. Yet she gives apostolic oversight to one of the world's most prominent organizations of Christian women. Fifty state Aglow presidents look to her for covering in the United States, as do national presidents of Aglow units in 150 other nations. Jane's apostolic authority applies to their activities related to Aglow, although it might also be a bit broader in certain individual cases.

Another example is Chris Hayward of Cleansing Stream, also a member of ICA. He has done more to set in place deliverance ministry teams in local churches than anyone else, to my knowledge. Over 2,500 churches in the U.S. and over 500 churches in 22 other countries are actively offering the Cleansing Stream Seminar. A significant number of these churches have at least one, and sometimes multiple, deliverance ministry teams developed and functioning under the covering of the local church pastor. Team members and leaders first experience the Seminar and Retreat themselves, and then ultimately enter the second year Cleansing Stream Discipleship Program. Leaders of this enormous international movement look to Chris Hayward as their functional apostle (though many have not yet become accustomed to using the title).

I could mention others, such as Loren Cunningham, who provides apostolic leadership to Youth With A Mission; Dick

Eastman, who heads Every Home for Christ; Chuck Pierce, of the Global Apostolic Prayer Network; and many others. They are all functional apostles in that role, not over churches or pastors, but over different dynamic movements that help advance the kingdom of God.

### Congregational Apostles

My primary area of academic expertise happens to be the field of church growth. Years of extensive research have brought me to the conclusion that there are only two predictable numerical barriers to the growth of a local church: the 200 barrier and the 700 to 800 barrier (numbers indicating active members). The vast majority—something like 90 percent—of American churches have fewer than 200 members, and 7 to 8 percent have between 200 and 700 to 800. That leaves 2 or 3 percent of churches with over 700 to 800 members.

Crossing each one of these barriers, with the church continuing to grow beyond those numbers, is a function of leadership more than anything else. Although many factors enter the equation for breaking the 200 barrier,[2] the major change in leadership involves the pastor's agreeing to become a "rancher" instead of a "shepherd." A shepherd offers one-on-one care to all parishioners, and this model, when other conditions are right, can get a church up to 200. But over 200 the pastor needs to begin delegating pastoral care to others. The rancher does not personally care for the sheep, but he or she is responsible for making sure it gets done. Due to the fact that this change in ministry style is next to impossible for most pastors to initiate and for most congregations to accept, 90 percent of churches will remain under the 200 barrier.

A few, however, will lead the church as ranchers, cross 200, and then plateau out somewhere around 700 to 800. Again, moving beyond 700 to 800 requires a special kind of leader. Back in

1980, America's foremost parish consultant, Lyle Schaller, suggested that a church of over 700 could accurately be described as a "minidenomination."[3] In 1999, Gary McIntosh, another highly regarded church growth expert, used secular labels to describe pastoral leadership of several sizes of churches, calling pastors of churches over 800 "president."[4]

With these figures somewhere in the back of my mind, I was once discussing leadership roles with a prominent pastor. At the time, more than 6,000 people attended his church, and it was still growing. By that time, I had begun teaching and writing about apostles. Suddenly it dawned on me that the best term for the leader of a "minidenomination" like his was probably not "president" or "chairman," but rather "apostle." To use new wineskin terminology, a "mini-apostolic network" might be a better description than "minidenomination." Given the fact that the average church in America has a Sunday attendance of around 85, an attendance of 6,000 would be the equivalent of something like 70 churches—a decent-sized apostolic network in itself.

As is the case with many, this particular pastor did not want to accept the title "apostle," even though he has started an ecclesiastical apostolic network. Using the title or not, this pastor's leadership role clearly fit under this category of "congregational apostle." As frequently happens, the church that the congregational apostle pastors also becomes the anchor church for his vertical apostolic network.

To summarize, a pastor can build a church to 200, a leader can take a church over 200, but it requires a congregational apostle to move the church past 700 to 800 and have it continue to grow vigorously.

## Four Activities of Horizontal Apostles

A major distinguishing characteristic of horizontal apostles is that, unlike vertical apostles, horizontal apostles do not ordinarily provide spiritual covering or direct ongoing personal accountability to those to whom they minister. Their anointing is in bringing together peers of one kind or another to accomplish certain purposes better than they could separately.

There are four subcategories, or activities, of horizontal apostles.

## Convening Apostles

This is the subcategory of apostles that I can write about in the first person. I see myself, much like James of Jerusalem, as a horizontal apostle with "convening" as my primary activity. Those of us who serve as convening apostles have been given an anointing to call together peer-level Christian leaders who minister in a defined field on a regular basis. We have the ability to form relational organizations for specific purposes as God directs.

For several years now I have been apostling the following groups:

- *Apostolic Council for Educational Accountability (ACEA).* This organization was formed to provide the educational institutions in the New Apostolic Reformation a creative functional substitute for traditional academic accreditation, which is seen by many as a dead-end road and a hindrance to being all that God wants us to be. Each May, educators representing some 70 schools and many apostolic networks come together to build relationships, share information, and encourage one another.

- *Apostolic Council of Prophetic Elders (ACPE).* An invitation-only group of up to 25 recognized prophets who gather together each September to build relationships, share what they are hearing prophetically, and hold themselves accountable to one another for quality and integrity in their prophetic ministries.

• *International Society of Deliverance Ministers (ISDM).* This group affords an annual opportunity for over 150 qualified and personally invited deliverance ministers (who had previously operated independently from one another) to gather each fall, build relationships, encourage one another, share mutual concerns, and learn together.

• *International Coalition of Apostles (ICA).* Over 500 apostles, having passed through a strict nomination and invitation process, belong to ICA. I preside over an annual meeting held in Dallas the first week of December. Apostles gather to hear from each other, connect for ministry opportunities, and get their finger on the pulse of what the Spirit is saying to the churches.

• *Eagles' Vision Apostolic Team (EVAT).* As I was organizing these horizontal networks, it gradually became clear that God was also asking me to provide a more vertical type of primary apostolic accountability to a small number of apostles, but not to their respective churches, networks or ministries. EVAT, therefore, is somewhere in between a horizontal and a vertical network (one member suggested that it might be "diagonal"!).

With the exception of EVAT, my apostolic authority over the members of the groups functions basically in calling and presiding over the annual meetings. I do not provide the members primary personal accountability, although I do provide secondary accountability because as the leader I am responsible for who is or is not a member. When I receive complaints or accusations against a member of any of my networks, I conscientiously investigate the charges. For example, I have dismissed four members of ICA and accepted the suggested resignation of others.

### Ambassadorial Apostles

Ambassadorial apostles have itinerant ministries that catalyze and nurture apostolic movements on a broad scale. They can do this on a national, regional or international arena. John Kelly of Ft. Worth, Texas, serves with me in the leadership team of ICA as an ambassadorial apostle. Suppose, for example, that a member of ICA in some part of the country wants to call together the apostles of the region in order to connect with each other and to strategize for the future. To make this happen, it is often wise to call in an outsider who may be able, among other things, to neutralize whatever negative church politics might have arisen in that area. I am generally not available for this kind of ministry, but John Kelly is. He is often the catalyst necessary to convene regional apostolic summits, and even to assist new apostles in organizing their apostolic networks properly.

Not only can an ambassadorial apostle help convene regional or international apostolic summits, but he or she is also available for troubleshooting existing apostolic movements. Since one of the qualities of apostolic ministry is to "set things in order," as Paul told Titus to do (see Titus 1:5), ambassadorial apostles often receive divine revelation as to what action needs to be taken at a certain time and place. They are frequently able to turn a lose-lose situation into a win-win victory to the glory of God.

### Mobilizing Apostles

Like ambassadorial apostles, mobilizing apostles are very willing to spend time on the road. They differ from ambassadorial apostles, however, in their focus on a specific cause or project. For example, Cindy Jacobs of Generals International travels the world meeting with movers and shakers, whom she calls "generals." Her focus is social transformation or reformation.

From time to time she invites them to gather together, usually in Washington, DC. When she does, her horizontal apostolic anointing takes effect and large numbers of generals travel from different nations to pray, share, hear what the Spirit is saying, and strategize for extending the kingdom of God. Jacobs is a classic mobilizing apostle.

**Territorial Apostles**

Some apostles have one of their primary apostolic spheres defined by a certain geographic territory. These territorial apostles have been given a great deal of authority within a city, state, nation or region. Not only have they themselves accepted the responsibility that God has given them within that territory, but Christian leaders and even some secular leaders have also recognized and affirmed the extraordinary influence that they have in that segment of society.

Two of the most outstanding territorial apostles with whom I am in contact are Bart Pierce, in the city of Baltimore, Maryland, and John Benefiel, in the state of Oklahoma. Bart Pierce, for example, was publicly commissioned a bishop/apostle by a consortium of pastors representing the African-American churches of Baltimore. John Benefiel, in turn, was publicly awarded the honor of a Cheyenne name by the Southern Cheyenne in Oklahoma, the state that hosts the largest concentration of Native Americans in the nation.

I do not believe God gives exclusive territorial jurisdiction to any one apostle. Bart Pierce is only one of several territorial apostles in Baltimore, and John Benefiel likewise in the state of Oklahoma.

A subset of territorial apostles includes apostles who are given apostolic leadership over certain ethnic groups. Biblical examples would be Peter and Paul. The most prominent ethnic division in their day was between Jews and Gentiles. God assigned Peter as an apostle to the "circumcision"—that is, the Jews—and He assigned Paul as an apostle to the "uncircumcision," the Gentiles (see Gal. 2:7). Both of them ministered in the same geographical areas, such as Galatia and Asia, but one primarily to Jews and the other primarily to Gentiles. An example of that today would be the difference between Dan Juster and me. Both of us are members of the Apostolic Council of ICA and both of us have ministry in the U.S. However, Dan ministers primarily to Jews and I minister primarily to Gentiles.

## Hyphenated Apostles

Many apostles have spiritual gifts, ministries and activities assigned by God that cover more than one category, and have been given other gifts (and even offices) alongside their gift and office of apostle. For example, I have the gift of teaching. For most of my ministry I considered "teacher" as my only office. Then I began to recognize that God had also given me the gift of apostle; so I considered myself a teacher *hyphen* apostle. Teaching was primary and apostling secondary. More recently, however, I would characterize myself as an apostle-teacher. A tangible indicator of this change would be financial. For 30 years I received my salary from Fuller Seminary as a teacher. Now I receive my salary from Eagles Vision Apostolic Team (EVAT) as an apostle.

Bill Hamon, one of the nation's most recognized prophets, describes himself as a prophet-apostle (as opposed to apostle-prophet). Michael Fletcher, the apostle over Grace Churches International of Fayetteville, North Carolina, is also senior pastor of Manna Church. He is an apostle-pastor.

Those who are recognized as apostles may also have more than one ministry or activity as I have defined them above. It is possible, for example, to be both a vertical and a horizontal apostle, although this is relatively rare. Mel Mullen of Red Deer, Canada, is an outstanding example. For years he was only a vertical, ecclesiastical apostle over his Word of Life network of churches. More recently, however, he has also emerged as the apostle most anointed to bring together other apostles in Canada in a horizontal apostolic network, the Canadian Coalition of Apostles.

Apostles are far from being all the same. In God's kingdom today we have many apostles who exercise their ministry in many spheres. We all fit someplace. It's helpful to know where.

**Notes**
1. C. Peter Wagner, *Churchquake!* (Ventura, CA: Regal Books, 1999), pp. 141-143.
2. For details on breaking the 200 barrier, see Part 1 "Overcoming Small Church Barriers of 200 People by C. Peter Wagner," *The Everychurch Guide to Growth* by Elmer Towns, C. Peter Wagner and Thom Rainer (Nashville, TN: Broadman & Holman Publishers, 1998), pp. 21-70.
3. Lyle E. Schaller, *The Multiple Staff and the Larger Church* (Nashville, TN: Abingdon Press, 1980), p. 28.
4. Gary L. McIntosh, *One Size Doesn't Fit All* (Grand Rapids, MI: Fleming H. Revell, 1999), p. 65.

# CHAPTER EIGHT

# APOSTLES
# IN THE
# WORKPLACE

I could not have written this chapter on apostles in the workplace before 2004—which isn't that long ago. In fact it was only in 2001 that my eyes started to open to the fact that there was even such a thing as a church in the workplace. I had been hearing some things about ministry in the workplace from some of my friends previous to that, but I had little personal interest in it. For the better part of 10 years, I had been concentrating on what I've written about in this book so far, namely, the biblical government of the church, apostles and prophets, and the New Apostolic Reformation. I was traditionally a church person, not a business or marketplace person. I was happy that others, not I, would be taking care of things like that.

## Intimidated by the Marketplace

The switch began in 2001 when a Christian business couple whom I had come to know, Dennis and Megan Doyle of Minneapolis, surprised me by inviting me to speak in the Twin Cities to a group of businesspeople who had been convening for some time. My first inclination was to send apologies since I had no experience in relating to this kind of an audience. I was used to speaking to church leaders, not to marketplace leaders. By then I had written five books on apostles and prophets, all targeted to church leaders. To be honest, I was a bit intimidated by the thought of addressing secular businesspeople.

As I was contemplating this invitation and praying about it, God got my attention by speaking directly to me in such a way that there was no doubt in my mind whom I was hearing. God said, "Son, I want you to pay strict attention to ministry in the marketplace!" From that moment on, the issue was no longer inclination or intimidation; it was obedience. So I said yes to God and told the Doyles that I would do it.

I had to come up with a plan on how to proceed. I didn't have any prepared teaching material on the subject. Since I am a professional scholar, my natural inclination was to begin to read what others had already found out. I began purchasing and reading books. Eventually, my personal library grew to over 100 volumes, but back then it was just a few. One of the books was John Beckett's *Loving Monday*. In it, he put his finger on a serious deficiency in my thinking. He convinced me that I had been thinking with a Greek mind-set when, as a believer, I should have been geared up to a Hebrew mind-set. As I wrestled through the issue, I came to realize that I had been thinking in a Greek way because that is what I had been taught by my professors in seminary.

## Greek Mind-set vs. Hebrew Mind-set

John Beckett argued his point by bringing up two famous Greek philosophers. The first was Protagoras. Beckett wrote, "Without the God of the Bible, human beings are left with only themselves. Protagoras, in the fifth century B.C., put it crisply when he offered his famous maxim, 'Man is the measure of all things.'"[1]

The second philosopher was Plato. Beckett wrote, "The Greeks couldn't get away from the concept of 'dualism'—the idea of higher and lower planes of ideas and activities. Plato was the clearest on this. He sought to identify unchanging universal truths, placing them in the higher of two distinct realms. The upper level he called 'form,' consisting of eternal ideas. The lower he called 'matter.' This lower realm was temporal and physical. Plato's primary interest lay in the higher form. He deemed it superior to the temporary and imperfect world of matter. The rub comes when we see where Plato placed work and occupations. Where, indeed? In the lower realm."[2]

This is exactly how I had been trained to regard work. It was a necessity of life for earning a living. It was something that believers should try to do well. But it was a low road compared to the high road of Christian ministry. My mind had been programmed to distinguish between:

- Spiritual vs. worldly
- Sacred vs. secular
- Church vs. world
- Clergy vs. laity

What I had not realized was that the Bible is not written from a Greek worldview but from a Hebrew one! Greek thinking tends to compartmentalize and stratify all of life. On the other hand, Hebrew thinking tends to integrate and connect all of life. Greeks see very little relationship between cosmic forces and daily life. Hebrews think that cosmic forces and daily life are interacting constantly. We traditional Christians believe the Hebrew-oriented Bible, but our Greek side wants to separate the secular and sacred. When we do this, work falls into the "secular" category, while Christian ministry falls into the "sacred."

For Hebrews, on the other hand, both work and ministry honor God. Interestingly enough, the Hebrew word for worship, *avodah*, is also translated "work" in the Bible. Imagine the concept of work being a form of worship!

## The Jewish Phenomenon

Consider what Steven Silbiger brings to light in his book *The Jewish Phenomenon*: "For Jews, wealth is a good thing, a worthy and respectable goal to strive toward. What's more, once you earn it, it is tragic to lose it. Judaism has never considered poverty a virtue. The first Jews were not poor, and that was good. The Jewish founding fathers, Abraham, Isaac, and Jacob, were blessed with cattle and land in abundance. Asceticism and self-denial are not Jewish ideals. With your financial house in order, it is easier to pursue your spiritual life."[3]

It goes without saying that this is vastly different from traditional Christian attitudes toward wealth. In fact, I believe that the Body of Christ in general has been under the spell of a pernicious spirit of poverty that has been passed through the generations since the monastic movement of the Middle Ages. We will not be able to grasp the dignity of work and wealth until we are delivered, individually and collectively, from this evil spirit.

How can we be delivered? Romans 12:2 makes clear that we can be transformed by the renewing of our minds. We need to think differently. We need to start by shifting our mental paradigm from the Greek worldview to the Hebrew worldview.

Here is something that may encourage us to think differently. Look at these remarkable statistics on Jewish-Americans, who comprise only 2 percent of the American population:

- The percentage of Jewish households with income greater than $50,000 is double that of non-Jews.
- The percentage of Jewish households with income less than $20,000 is half that of non-Jews.
- Forty-five percent of the top 40 of the Forbes 400 richest Americans are Jewish.
- One-third of American multimillionaires are Jewish.
- Twenty percent of professors at leading universities are Jewish.
- Forty percent of partners in the leading law firms in New York and Washington are Jewish.
- Twenty-five percent of all American Nobel prize winners are Jewish.[4]
- Less than 0.1 percent of American prison inmates are Jewish.

When we see figures like that, we naturally ask the question, "What is going on?" The answer is that they think like God! In other words Jews have a Hebrew mind-set. They are not under the oppression of a Greek-oriented monastic heritage like most of us Christians are.

## Beyond the Local Church

If we are going to understand how apostles function in the workplace, we need to realize that God's plan for His people extends far beyond the four walls of the local church.

Our Greek mind-set has caused us to fall into the trap of what Ed Silvoso, author of *Anointed for Business*, calls "four lethal misbeliefs" concerning church ministry and business:

1. There is a God-ordained division between clergy and laity.
2. The Church is called to operate primarily inside a building referred to as a temple.
3. People involved in business cannot be as spiritual as those serving in traditional Church ministry.
4. The primary role of marketplace Christians is to make money to support the vision of those "in the ministry."[5]

As we renew our minds concerning God's love for the workplace, we will distance ourselves further and further from such traditional ideas.

## The Kingdom of God

One of the debilitating tendencies to which many Christians have been subject is in identifying the kingdom of God with the church. They are not the same. The kingdom of God includes the church but goes far beyond it. The kingdom of God exists wherever there are those for whom Jesus is their ultimate King. It has no geographical or political boundaries! That's why Jesus said, in Luke 17:21, that the kingdom of God is within you.

God's vision is that His kingdom will come and His will be done on Earth as it is in heaven. That's what we're supposed to pray in the Lord's Prayer. Every one of us for whom Jesus is Lord is in turn expected to do our part in advancing God's kingdom. Some of what we do in advancing the kingdom of God will be done in the church. But much of it will be done outside of the church, in the workplace.

I have used the word "church" in its traditional sense, rather than as it exists in the workplace. That is another lethal misbelief derived from categorizing things in the Greek way! Thinking must be adjusted to understand that there is a church in the workplace as well as a church in the traditional form we are used to. By this I do not mean that there are two churches—there is only one true church of Jesus Christ. What I mean is that there are two distinct forms of the church: one that meets on Sundays and one that is in the workplace the other six days of the week.

## Church = *Ekklesia*

The reason I say there are two forms of Christ's one church goes back to the meaning of the original biblical word for church, *ekklesia*. After Jesus had been with His disciples for a year and a half, He said, "I will build my church [*ekklesia*]" (Matt. 16:18). The word *ekklesia* had certain political nuances in the society of the Roman Empire in those days, but Jesus gave the word a new meaning that would last for centuries. It was a word that would encompass all of His people: His church *body*. No political meaning was intended. *Ekklesia* means essentially "the people of God." Nothing more, nothing less.

Sometimes in the New Testament we find the word *ekklesia* used for God's people gathered together. However, an equal number of times it is used for God's people scattered wherever they might be. To put it in modern terminology, when God's people are gathered together in their local churches on Sunday, they are the true church. And when they go out to the workplace Monday through Saturday, they are still the true church.

The terminology I like best to describe these two different forms of the church is derived from the common sociological terminology "nuclear family" and "extended family." The nuclear family lives under the same roof. The extended family, including uncles, aunts, cousins, grandparents and in-laws, gets together when people have family reunions. It is the same family, but the forms it takes are different.

Once we realize that the extended church is a form of the real church, some interesting implications arise. One concerns church government. The foundation of the church, according to Ephesians 2:20, is apostles and prophets. Up until now, we have associated apostles and prophets with the nuclear church, but there is no logical reason to think that church government stops there. Why not apostles and prophets in the extended church as well?

So let's take biblical church government to its logical conclusion. Let's agree that there are workplace apostles.

## The Cultural Gap

Are there similarities and differences between nuclear church apostles and workplace apostles? Yes, there would be some differences, because each of the two forms of the church has a different culture. And, although the thought might make some people uncomfortable, the cultural gap between the two is much larger than we might think.

This was confirmed by two social scientists, Laura Nash and Scotty McLennan, who conducted a huge research project and published their results in a very important book titled *Church on Sunday, Work on Monday*. They didn't use the terms "nuclear church" and "extended church," but obviously "church on Sunday" would be the nuclear church and "work on Monday" would be the extended church.

For example, Nash and McLennan found that "businesspeople and clergy live in two worlds. Between the two groups lie minefields seeded with attitudes about money, poverty, and the spirit of business."[6] Here is how bad it can get: "The clergy tended to represent business as an aggregate concept, centered on money or profit—code words for excessive wealth and exploitation. They saw businesspeople as greedy and selfish; they repeatedly mentioned money as business's primary concern (excessive salaries, consumption lifestyles, materialistic ambitions, the wage gap). Accumulation of wealth had especially negative associations of idolatry, sin, materialism, false values, wrong priorities, selfishness, and most of all injustice against the poor."[7]

One of the underlying problems is that these two cultures, like any human culture, have different rulebooks. Extended church leaders, by and large, know both rulebooks. They follow the extended-church rulebook Monday through Saturday, then shift to the nuclear-church rulebook on Sunday when they go to church. In anthropological terms, they are bicultural. However, most nuclear church leaders know only one rulebook, namely, their own. They are monocultural. The rub for monocultural people comes when they judge behavior and attitudes of others as right or wrong based on their own rulebook. That can cause strong reactions, like those quoted in the Nash and McLennan book.

In order for us to move ahead into our destiny as one church in two forms, it is essential that both sides not only understand but affirm the other's rulebook. This will take time. My book *The Church in the Workplace* steers things in the right direction. In the second part of the book is a list of eight of the rules that typically have different interpretations in the nuclear church than in the extended church. The eight rules include ministers in the workplace, apostles in the workplace, influence and authority, time management, stewardship, new forms of the church, the means and the end, and tough calls.

## Christian Ministry

Take for example the concept of Christian ministry, sometimes referred to as "full-time Christian service." The general idea—which I bought into for most of my career—was that all ministry had to be done in connection with programs and activities associated with the nuclear church. People would often say, "The Lord called me to leave my job and go into the ministry." That reflects nuclear-church rulebook thinking.

On the other hand, the extended-church rulebook sees work as a legitimate ministry as well. This view is based on the biblical word *diakonia*, which is translated as "ministry." However, in the New Testament, *diakonia* is translated as "ministry" only about half the time; the other half it is translated as "service." This means that if you are serving people on your job, then you are ministering. Airplane pilots minister to their passengers. Restaurant servers minister to their customers. Nurses minister to their patients. Gardeners minister to homeowners. CEOs minister to their stockholders. And on and on.

This greatly expands the concept of "equipping the saints for the work of the ministry" (Eph. 4:12). Who is supposed to be doing this? According to Ephesians 4:11, apostles, prophets, evangelists, pastors and teachers are. But how much could typical nuclear-church leaders equip their saints for ministry in the workplace? Not very much! Because they haven't been trained for it. Not only that, but very few of them have had in-depth experience in the workplace.

Workplace apostles are the ones who have the ability to set things in order in the workplace and equip the saints there according to the rules of the extended-church rulebook.

## Luke, a Workplace Apostle

Let's go back to 2001 when I was first invited to speak to workplace leaders. Once God set me on the path of getting involved with ministry in the marketplace and I started thinking things through, I began to wonder about the possibility of workplace apostles. One of the first questions was whether such a thing would be biblical. I was comfortable with Paul as a prototype of a nuclear-church apostle, so I started a search for a biblical workplace apostle. By that time I had written my commentary on the book of Acts, *Acts of the Holy Spirit*, which may be why Luke came to my mind. The more I looked into it, the more convinced I became that Luke, as well as Lydia, provided a biblical prototype of a workplace apostle.

Both Luke and Lydia were prominent in the workplace. Luke was a physician and Lydia had an import-export business (as indicated by the fact that she was a "seller of purple"). They were both God-fearing Gentiles. By all indications, they were wealthy—an important source of authority in the extended church. Undoubtedly one of the many house churches that had been planted in Philippi would have met in Lydia's house. In all probability, Luke and Lydia could have been apostolic leaders for the churches in all of Macedonia.

## Paul's True Companion

Not only were Luke and Lydia probably church leaders, but they also kept in touch with Paul and helped support his ministry. Paul's letter to the Philippians is essentially a thank-you letter for the money they sent. He addresses it to his "true companion" or "true yokefellow" (see Phil. 4:3), which most commentators suggest is Luke. Paul writes, "When I departed from Macedonia, no church shared with me concerning giving and receiving but you only" (Phil. 4:15).

Contrary to much misguided thinking, contributing money to ministries is not the only role that workplace apostles have. Luke is an excellent example. Not only was he a leader of the church in Philippi that he helped plant, but he traveled extensively with Paul as a colleague on mission trips. He went to Philippi with Paul (see Acts 16:10-18). He went from Philippi to Troas to Miletus (see Acts 20:5-21). He went from Jerusalem to Rome (see Acts 27:1–28:16). Twice he visited Paul in prison (see Col. 4:14 and 2 Tim. 4:9-11).

Perhaps the greatest apostolic credential that Luke had was being inspired by the Holy Spirit to write over 25 percent of the New Testament. Nothing in the New Testament would indicate that there is anything spiritually inferior on the part of workplace apostles. In fact, it is noteworthy that Luke, the prototype of a workplace apostle, wrote the same percentage of the New Testament as Paul, the prototype of a nuclear-church apostle!

## Characteristics of Workplace Apostles

Spiritually, then, workplace apostles and nuclear-church apostles are on the same plane. In matters of extraordinary character, the requirements for one are just as high as for the other. Most normal apostolic ministries would be observed in both.

However, because they operate under different rulebooks, some different characteristics of workplace apostles are evident:

- *Respect.* Among nuclear-church apostles, influence derives largely from relationships; whereas for extended-church apostles, influence derives primarily from respect. In the nuclear church, respect is earned through relationships: relationship with God, relationships with other believers, relationships with peers. In the workplace, relationships follow respect. People will recognize the authority of a workplace apostle if they command respect from associates and if their track record authenticates their effectiveness in their field of endeavor.

- *Money.* Although it is not the only consideration, money is one of the major factors commanding respect in the workplace. Access to financial resources builds credibility and confers authority more in the workplace than in the nuclear church. While accumulation of money must never be an end in itself, it nevertheless is a useful tool for extending the kingdom of God. Here is how Rich Marshall puts it: "We need to start thinking about authority outside traditional interpretations—and not just who can exert authority, but the tools that go with it. For example, consider money. For years, money has borne the image of 'filthy lucre' (especially in the church world). Yet, money is a tool God gives to businesspersons to gain authority in their city—which means money to carry out tasks that will benefit society."[8] Workplace apostles who are financially independent have an advantage over those who are dependent on others for their income.

- *Risk taker.* The road leading to apostolic authority in the workplace is a minefield. Along with notable successes, workplace apostles have become accustomed to taking serious hits. Most have lost much money. In fact, many can tell stories about how they lost it all. These experiences have not deterred them. They regard them as learning opportunities. For every step they get knocked back, they move two steps forward. They are ready to take more risks. By God's grace they fear no one; and they do not turn back.

- *Renaissance person.* Another criterion for respect in the workplace is being perceived as a "Renaissance person." These are individuals who have command of a broad spectrum of interests. They have accumulated skills and experiences in a number of different fields, giving them a large reservoir from which to draw for solving problems. This ability brings with it a good deal of authority.

- *Negotiating legal structures.* Workplace apostles intuitively move through and around legal entanglements. To put it in the vernacular, they know how to wheel and deal. They do not allow legal structures to set unnecessary boundaries around what God can do. They know how to cut through red tape, using inter-workings of relationships that have been carefully built through the years based on mutual trust. They have a slogan: It's not what you know, it's who you know.

- *Position of influence.* Authority also comes from the unusual influence one has earned in his or her determined sphere of the workplace. The seven molders of culture include: family, religion, government, arts, media, business and education. Each of these has numerous subdivisions, and all have specific rule-books as to how influence is attained. Workplace apostles will know what their sphere or spheres are, and they will have attained positions of influence within those spheres. The explicit overriding motivation for their use of influence is to glorify God.

• *Kingdom mind-set.* Not every financially successful Christian leader in the workplace is necessarily an apostle. Those who are apostles, however, will have a Kingdom mentality—meaning that their driving passion is to see God's kingdom values permeate society on every level. They exhibit the expected characteristics of any apostle. They are actively involved in city or nation transformation as well as setting in order the "church" located in the workplace.

**Notes**

1. John D. Beckett, *Loving Monday* (Downers Grove, IL: InterVarsity Press, 1998), p. 66.
2. Ibid., p. 67.
3. Steven Silbiger, *The Jewish Phenomenon* (Atlanta, GA: Longstreet Press, Inc., 2000), p. 15.
4. Information paraphrased from the above, p. 4.
5. Ed Silvoso, *Anointed for Business* (Ventura, CA: Regal Books, 2002), p. 23.
6. Laura Nash and Scotty McLennan, *Church on Sunday, Work on Monday* (San Francisco, CA: Jossey-Bass, 2001), p. 128.
7. Ibid., p. 129.
8. Rich Marshall, *God@Work, Volume 2* (Shippensburg, PA: Destiny Image, 2005), pp. 66-67.

# CHAPTER NINE

# APOSTLES
# FOR
# SOCIAL
# TRANSFORMATION

## Our Goal: Social Transformation

Through the 1980s, most of us charismatically inclined evangelicals thought that fulfilling the Great Commission would largely be measured by the number of souls saved and the number of churches multiplied.

This assumption began to change during the 1990s, when the idea that the kingdom of God is not confined to the four walls of the local church began to take hold strongly among Christian leaders. We began to take our prayer, "Your kingdom come, Your will be done on earth as it is in heaven," much more seriously than we had in the past. We believed that not only did God desire to save the lost and bring them into our churches, but that He also desired to change for better the world in which we live.

Some of us began to talk about "city taking" and "city reaching" and "changing culture." But gradually, toward the end of the decade, "social transformation" seemed to be the most satisfactory way of expressing our outreach goal. The renowned *Transformations* video, produced by George Otis Jr.'s Sentinel Group, helped sharpen our thinking. "Social transformation" includes all of the other terms, but it is broader. It encompasses spiritual transformation (both church growth and public morality), economic transformation, educational transformation, family transformation, transformation of the media and the arts, and governmental transformation. This can be applied to neighborhoods, cities, regions and nations.

It seems that the most manageable unit of all is probably the city, so I will focus on city transformation in this chapter.

## Our Premise: Territorial Apostles

The major purpose of this book is to affirm that there are individuals today who have been given the gift and office of apostle just as there were in biblical times. This implies that, among other things, they have been entrusted with an extraordinary amount of spiritual authority in the Body of Christ. But this authority only functions under divine anointing when it is exercised within the apostle's God-assigned sphere(s).

Knowing this highlights the importance of understanding apostolic spheres as much as possible. One of the spheres in which some apostles serve the Body of Christ is territorial. Thus, it is proper to surmise that we have territorial apostles among us. A few biblical examples of territorial spheres are:

## Paul

Paul suggests to the Corinthians that he does not consider himself an apostle to the whole world or to the whole Body of Christ. "We, however," he says, "will not boast [referring to boasting about apostolic authority as mentioned a few verses earlier in 2 Cor. 10:8] beyond measure, but within the limits of the sphere which God appointed us—a sphere which especially includes you" (2 Cor. 10:13). Corinth was a city in the Roman province of Achaia. Other provinces that we know were also included in Paul's apostolic sphere of authority were Macedonia, Asia and Galatia. Paul's sphere would not include places like Alexandria, Jerusalem or Rome or any number of other cities or provinces where churches had by then been planted.

## Titus

Titus, a member of Paul's apostolic team, operated as an apostle in the territory of Crete. Paul writes to him, "For this reason I left you in Crete, that you should set in order the things that are lacking, and appoint elders in every city as I commanded you" (Titus 1:5).

Titus might well have had other territorial spheres as well. His name is frequently mentioned in connection with Corinth. Paul had sent him there as a troubleshooter; and Paul writes back to them from Philippi, saying, "Nevertheless God, who comforts the downcast, comforted us by the coming of Titus" (2 Cor. 7:6). Paul's obvious relief suggests that Titus probably did some fruitful apostolic work in Corinth.

There is also a strong hint in Paul's last epistle that another of Titus's territorial spheres could have been Dalmatia (see 2 Tim. 4:9).

### Peter

Likewise, Peter lists what are undoubtedly his own major territorial jurisdictions when he writes 1 Peter. He begins the letter, "Peter, an apostle of Jesus Christ, to the pilgrims of the Dispersion in Pontus, Galatia, Cappadocia, Asia, and Bithynia" (1 Pet. 1:1).

## Cultural Spheres

Note that in 1 Peter 1:1, Peter doesn't mention Achaia or Macedonia, which were two of Paul's spheres. However, he *does* mention the other two of Paul's provinces, Galatia and Asia. This could lead us to deduce that within *territorial* spheres there can also be *cultural* spheres. Look at the words in Peter's greeting: "to the pilgrims of the Dispersion." This means that his epistle is directed not to the Gentiles, but specifically to the Diaspora Jews who were located in the five provinces he mentions. Paul, who was an apostle to the *uncircumcision*, was assigned to the *Gentiles* who lived in Galatia and Asia. Peter, who was an apostle to the *circumcision*, was assigned to the *Jews* who lived in the same provinces.

## City Transformation

With this in mind, let's take a look at the state of affairs with regard to our efforts across America toward city transformation.

The widespread interest in city transformation began in 1990 with the publication of John Dawson's bestseller, *Taking Our Cities for God*. During the decade of the 1990s, virtually every major city in America launched a city transformation project of one kind or another. Some of the finest of the nation's Christian leadership was involved up-front. A quality library emerged with authors such as Francis Frangipane, Ed Silvoso, George Otis, Jr., Jack Dennison, Jack Hayford, Frank Damazio, and many others joining in to help point the way. Mission America, under the leadership of Paul Cedar, launched a major nationwide project aimed at city transformation.

It looked to many of us as if the 1990s would see tangible answers to the prayer "Thy kingdom come" in city after city. But it didn't happen. In fact, after now more than 15 years of intense effort, it would be difficult to pinpoint a city or even a smaller community in America that has been transformed as a result of proactive, strategic planning. One result of this is that we seem to be experiencing some disturbing sort of transformation fatigue, with some leaders beginning to throw their hands up in despair.

## Persevering Leadership

The front-line researcher for social transformation has been George Otis, Jr. A major vehicle for his reports are documentary videos. His first video, *Transformations*, sparked powerful movements for changing society in many parts of the world. In that video he reports on four cities in various stages of transformation. One of them, Almolonga, Guatemala, unquestionably deserved to be classified as "transformed" in the sense that it likely would be so described by a disinterested sociologist.

One of George Otis's extremely useful discoveries was a list of five commonalities of cities experiencing significant stages of transformation. They are (1) persevering leadership; (2) fervent, united prayer; (3) social reconciliation; (4) public power encounters; and (5) diagnostic research (spiritual mapping). The first two were common to all the cities researched, and the last three were common to 90 percent.

I want to focus on the first commonality, persevering leadership, in an attempt to show that territorial apostles are essential for successful, proactive social transformation.

## Theological Compass Points

The accelerated and widespread efforts toward city transformation in the 1990s revealed what I would consider three theological compass points that now help mold our thinking about the way we develop strategies for our cities. Notice that each one carries an important "however," which serves as a mild disclaimer:

- *Unity of the Body of Christ is a prerequisite for social transformation.* However, we have also discovered that not just any unity will do. We can end up with either functional unity or dysfunctional unity (which I'll come back to later).

- *The church of the city or region is spiritually one church with multiple congregations.* However, the idea of the city church can be unwisely applied, precipitating debilitating egalitarianism. (Also more on that later.)

- *The foundation of the church is apostles and prophets* (see Eph. 2:20). However, this applies to city transformation through two distinct apostolic roles: apostles of the *nuclear* church and apostles of the *extended* church or workplace.

## Apostles—Not Pastors—Are the Gatekeepers

*City transformation will rise or fall on persevering leadership.* This pivotal phrase, which I have italicized, combines verbiage from my friends John Maxwell and George Otis, Jr. Even if we have everything else in place, our efforts will fizzle if we lack the God-anointed leadership.

If this is true (and I believe it is), then a central question becomes, Who are the God-appointed leaders or spiritual gatekeepers of the city? I am afraid that we reached a misguided answer to this question in the 1990s. Our assumption then was that the local church pastors were the spiritual gatekeepers of the city. I even carried this questionable idea into some of the books I wrote during that season.

One reason why many agreed with this conclusion in the 1990s is that back then we were only beginning to learn about apostles. We knew there was a church of the city all right, but we were not mature enough to understand that the God-given foundation of that church is apostles and prophets (see Eph. 2:20). Nor was the governmental order clear to us: "*First* apostles, *second* prophets, *third* teachers" (1 Cor. 12:28, emphasis added). We were actually getting it backward! Since most pastors who preach weekly sermons function also as teachers, they fit quite well into the third category. Biblically, however, 1 Corinthians 12:28 shows that the true spiritual gatekeepers of the city would be apostles, not pastors (or teachers).

Of all the different kinds of apostles, it is the territorial apostles who would be the ones most likely to provide the persevering leadership that is required for city transformation.

## Weaknesses of the Pastoral Approach

Not only is it unbiblical to assume that pastors would be the spiritual gatekeepers of a city, but, looking back, we realize that this concept has not worked well in practice. Our disappointing experiences during the decade of the 1990s have uncovered three practical weaknesses to the pastoral approach:

1. *Misapplying the valid concept of the city church.* When we began to agree that the church of the city was one church with multiple congregations, we then made the serious mistake of assuming that all local church pastors were therefore "co-pastors" of the city church. This meant that pastors who were ineffective (sad to discover, but many were) had just as much to say about what to do and when to do it as the pastors who were good at what they do. The upshot was that it tended to neutralize the leadership ability of the strongest leaders of the church in the city.

2. *The Billy Graham committee model.* For over 40 years, the most effective model for accomplishing a true citywide, interchurch project was the Billy Graham committee. It worked well for two reasons: It had strong leadership and a united vision. However, both the top leadership and the vision for the project were provided by an agency that was located *outside* of the city. The city pastors basically functioned not as the leaders but as the supporting cast for the leader, who would come to their city and hold meetings for a week or so. This worked well for one event, but it cannot work for long-term city transformation. For city transformation, a switch is needed from outside leadership to inside leadership, from event-orientation to process-orientation, and from administrative and diplomatic leaders to more aggressive, risk-taking leaders.

3. *The pastors' prayer summits.* In city after city, one of the
   most appealing ways to begin the process of city
   transformation seemed to be the pastors' prayer
   summit (originally designed by Joe Aldrich of
   Portland, Oregon). The premise was that if we could
   get the pastors of the city praying together, God
   would then respond and bring city transformation.
   That well-intentioned hope never fully materialized,
   for two reasons: (1) No one was allowed to come to
   the summit and present an agenda (such as city
   transformation or any other agenda) to the group,
   and (2) the focus was devotional and relational, but
   not task-oriented. The result was that we saw (and
   are still seeing) an unprecedented amount of united
   prayer in city after city, but without a united vision.
   No united vision, no social transformation!

## Functional and Dysfunctional Unity

No one whom I know would disagree with the premise that unity
of the Body of Christ is a divine prerequisite for city transformation. But not all have agreed on the form this unity should take.

I now see an important difference between two forms of
unity that I did not see in the 1990s:

1. *Pastoral unity.* Pastoral unity is mercy-motivated, relational, politically correct, polite and peaceful.
2. *Apostolic unity.* Apostolic unity is task-oriented, vision-
   ary, aggressive, warlike and often abrasive.

One of the major differences between the two is that in the
paradigm of pastoral unity, unity can (and almost inevitably
does) become an end in itself. In the paradigm of apostolic

unity, unity is only a means toward a higher end, which is the task at hand. Apostles will recognize that the perceived need for pastors to build personal relationships across unfamiliar social, racial, denominational, cultural, and church-size lines is good, but it should not be regarded as a prerequisite for social transformation. Apostles also know that a workable process for reaching the whole city does not require 100 percent of the church leaders, nor even a majority of them, in many cases.

## Apostolic Unity

While those who lean toward pastoral unity may find supporting Scripture, apostles will focus on texts such as Jesus' prayer in John 17:21, where He prays, "that they all may be one, as You, Father are in Me, and I in You; that they also may be one in Us, that the world may believe that You sent Me." Unity here is obviously not the end; world evangelization is. And whatever kind of unity that can be successful in helping implement world evangelization is the kind of unity that Jesus was praying for. Jesus actually said, "Do not think that I came to bring peace on earth. I did not come to bring peace but a sword" (Matt. 10:34).

This concept seems to play out fairly consistently in the history of the Church. The major movements of God throughout history generally did not produce unity in the Body of Christ, but rather they precipitated serious division. Take, for example, the Reformation with Martin Luther, the Methodists with John Wesley, the Presbyterians with John Knox, the Salvation Army with William Booth, or the Azusa Street revival, which initiated worldwide Pentecostalism. All of these movements were powerful, apostolic-type movements, with each precipitating substantial disunity in the Church as a whole.

Look at the cities that rank high on the scale of transformation (which George Otis, Jr. has researched). As a rule, they did not begin their transformation process only after a successful effort at unifying the churches of their region. Some did, but they are the exception, not the rule. Those who became persevering leaders of their cities more often than not first provoked division in their city—as apostolic leaders are prone to do.

Even though they did not begin this way, one of the final outcomes of these movements of God was unity. However, it was not typically a pastoral-type of unity. The resulting unity was usually shaped into a new wineskin, much to the consternation of some of those who insisted on remaining in the old wineskins.

## Hidden Costs of Pastoral Unity

The pastoral mind-set takes comfort in Scriptures such as, "Behold, how good and how pleasant it is for brethren to dwell together in unity" (Ps. 133:1). They like to meet together, eat together, pray together, confess their sins to one other, exchange pulpits, and love each other. These relationships may seem so much like the fruit of the Spirit that they can gradually acquire an aurora of Shekinah glory. And when that happens, meeting together can become something that must be preserved whatever the cost. Pastoral unity easily becomes a desirable end in itself.

However, one of the hidden costs of preserving this kind of pastoral gathering is avoiding whatever could be potentially divisive. This inevitably requires that the elements bonding the group together be reduced to the least common denominator. Consequently, it is common to see groups of pastors who are traditional, white, middle-class, Republican, denominational evangelicals. They would like to think that they represent the whole city, but most frequently they don't. Their leadership is typically consensus-building and maintenance-oriented. The chief duty of these leaders becomes to preserve the status quo in the most stimulating, easygoing way possible.

## Invisible Walls of Division

Ironically, ongoing groups of city leaders in which, to use a George Otis phrase, "courtesy trumps conviction" can unwittingly produce division. Rarely do these groups attract the active participation of the most creative and influential Christian leaders of the city. Some of them show up, at first motivated perhaps by a guilty conscience or feelings of religious obligation or a desire for local Christian unity. But soon they gradually self-exclude from the group—they're not driven out; they draw themselves out. They are repeatedly invited back, but they claim they don't have the time (despite the fact that members of hardly any other profession in the United States dispose of more personal discretionary time than do pastors!). The deep down issue is not time; it is *priority*.

Who, exactly, are those who tend to assign a low priority to, and exclude themselves from, citywide pastoral gatherings? There are at least six kinds of leaders who frequently turn out to have higher priorities:

1. *Vision-driven pastors.* These pastors tend to quickly become restless with patching up old wineskins and preserving the status quo.

2. *Task-oriented pastors and parachurch leaders.* They clearly see that prioritizing unity at all costs will not help them accomplish their task.

3. *Influential minority leaders.* They perceive that presence without power is a form of tokenism. Almost every citywide gathering includes some minority leaders who have a special grace to build bridges to other segments of society, but rarely are they the movers and shakers within their own minority communities.

4. *Pastors of dynamic, growing megachurches.* Their personal agendas are usually in a different solar system than the vast majority of the other pastors in the same city. The resulting communication gap is virtually impossible to surmount.

5. *Charismatic pastors.* The group typically embraces the distinctness of evangelical pastors without question, but requires that charismatic pastors check their own distinctness at the door in order to preserve the least common denominator. This makes the typical meeting more boring than some charismatics can handle!

6. *Apostles.* They find themselves outside of their apostolic spheres and consequently cannot function as apostles within the pastorally-oriented group.

When these six kinds of leaders do not show up, even after they are personally invited, the gossip starts. They may frequently be characterized as indifferent, on ego trips, empire builders, tooting their own horn, they don't believe in the church of the city, or that if they don't lead it, they don't join it. That last statement, by the way, is true when you think of it: They are *leaders*! Asking a leader to join a group but not lead is like asking a singer to join the choir and not sing.

One unfortunate result of this invisible wall of division is that the .300 hitters of the Christian leadership of the city are excluded from the starting lineup. Little wonder that we have seen few winners among American cities desirous of seeing the power of God manifested in social transformation.

## Can We Make a Switch?

Since our pastor-oriented approaches of the 1990s have not produced the expected results, can we switch to a new paradigm? Can we begin the process of recognizing that apostles are the foundation of the church in the city?

This brings up, once again, the crucial role of territorial apostles in social transformation. There are some important guidelines for identifying territorial apostles that I believe will be valuable for opening the needed doors toward recognizing and affirming them.

We must keep in mind that not all apostles *in* a city are also apostles *of* the city. Not all ecclesiastical apostles or functional apostles or mobilizing apostles or vertical apostles also have a *territorial* sphere. I am one case in point. I am an apostle who lives in Colorado Springs, Colorado, but God has not assigned my city to me as one of my operational apostolic spheres.

It is likewise important to recognize that every city, in all likelihood, will have several territorial apostles assigned to it, not just one. That means that different apostles *of* a given city will have different subspheres within the city. One apostle of the city, for example, may operate in the black community, another in the Hispanic community, and yet another in the white community. Just as in the province of Asia, Paul's sphere was Gentiles, and Peter's sphere was Jews.

Other subdivisions are likely, especially as the size of the city in question increases. Among nuclear-church apostles, one apostle might be recognized among evangelicals, for example, and another among charismatics. One's sphere might be in the northern part of the city, and another's in the south. Another's sphere might be the youth of the city. Then among workplace apostles, one might have a sphere involving government, one real estate, one the health care profession, one education, another media, and so forth.

## Territorial Commitment

How can we recognize who are the bona fide territorial apostles of our city? It goes without saying that they must exhibit the qualities of every apostle that I have been describing in this book. Beyond that, however, territorial apostles must pass the test of territorial commitment.

Bob Beckett of Hemet, California (one of the cities featured in the *Transformations* video), has written the textbook on territorial commitment, titled *Commitment to Conquer* (Grand Rapids, MI: Chosen Books, 1997). In it he makes a convincing argument that spiritual authority in a given region is proportional to the degree of territorial commitment of the Christian leader.

This applies first of all to local church pastors, who across the board (at least in America) exhibit a relatively low level of territorial commitment. What that means is that, as a starter, some 90 percent of American pastors do not expect to be in their present parish 10 years from now! For example, Southern Baptists, the largest denomination, shows an average pastoral tenure of only 2.7 years. United Methodist pastors (the second largest denomination) have a tenure of 3.4 years. And so on. Relatively few pastors have the same lifetime commitment to their community that most dentists, lawyers, automobile dealers, law enforcement officers, or general contractors have. That is an appalling reality. With such a short term, itinerant mind-set, how can a pastor make a long-term commitment to a community, a task, or even to setting a solid example of leadership for those around him or her?

Second, territorial commitment applies even more strictly to territorial apostles than it does to local church pastors. In my mind it would be just as difficult to imagine a blind surgeon or a stuttering radio announcer or an obese track star as it would be to imagine an apostle of the city not fully committed to the city.

## Three Fishing Pools

In light of this, what should we do?

It is not up to us to create apostles. Only God does that, by giving them the gift of apostle and assigning them their apostolic spheres. But it is definitely up to us to recognize the apostles that God has given to the church—both to the nuclear church and to the extended church. The people of God must encourage them, award them the office when appropriate, and submit gratefully to the authority of the apostle or apostles who are over whatever territorial sphere in which we find ourselves. When we do this, the government will be in place to receive the powerful outpouring of the Holy Spirit upon our cities, which will lead to social transformation on a worldwide scale.

As we begin to look for territorial apostles, let's look in the right places. I perceive that there are three major "fishing pools" in which we might be likely to find territorial apostles (though these are not the *only* three places where territorial apostles will be found). Furthermore, not all genuine apostles in these three fishing pools will have been assigned by God to be apostles *of* the city. Many of them will have other apostolic spheres. These three, however are a good place to start:

## Workplace Apostles

Leaning on what we saw in the last chapter, I have formed a strong opinion that the primary source for territorial apostles will be apostles in the workplace, not apostles in the nuclear church. For one thing, territorial commitment is a given. While there are exceptions, most workplace leaders who are mature enough to be recognized as apostles do not expect to move elsewhere. This produces significant spiritual authority. For another thing, workplace leaders have considerably more influence among the movers and shakers of the city than do nuclear-church leaders. They are the ones who have insider access to the principal molders of culture, such as government, business, education, media and arts. Finally, they control significant wealth. I am convinced that without access to wealth, we will see very little social transformation over the years.

During the 1990s, almost all our activity toward social transformation was in the hands of nuclear-church leaders. The active, influential, extended-church leader in our circles was the exception to the rule. We now must readjust our thinking if we are going to make the progress we hope for. Helping workplace apostles get into their rightful place might tend to irritate certain nuclear-church leaders, which is one of the reasons I wrote *The Church in the Workplace*. Part of the purpose of that book was to help the leaders of each of the two forms of the church to understand, appreciate and affirm the others.

## Megachurch Pastors

Among nuclear-church leaders, megachurch pastors would be the most likely fishing pool for territorial apostles.

Church growth research has shown that, across the board, the larger the church, the longer the pastoral tenure. Most pastors of churches of 1,000 or 2,000 or more have long since stopped looking for "greener pastures." They see their call to their congregation as a lifetime assignment. They have passed the test of territorial commitment. Furthermore, those among them who pastor dynamically growing (not stagnant or declining) megachurches would also fit the definition of "congregational apostles" (explained in chapter 7). The implication of this is that these pastors are both territorial *and* apostles.

### Parachurch Leaders

Not all parachurch leaders are apostles, but some are. Among them, some may have been assigned by God to the city in which they minister as their apostolic sphere. There may not be many, but they should not be overlooked simply on the premise that they lead their own ministries.

One of the better known parachurch leaders who is a territorial apostle is Doug Stringer of Somebody Cares in Houston, Texas. He has established a recognized track record of territorial commitment and effective ministry toward social transformation in Houston.

It's time that we switched from the pastoral approach to the apostolic approach if we are serious about transforming our cities and our society as a whole. It will not be an easy transition, but I believe that with the help of God it can be done, and relatively soon. If we do, there will be only winners. The kingdom of God will stand out more and more in the texture and fabric of our communities and of our nation.

# Chapter Ten

# CONCLUSION: NEW WINE IN NEW WINESKINS

The notion that there are apostles in today's Church is not yet common currency. Only a very small fraction of practicing pastors—mostly younger ones—were taught about apostles in their seminary or Bible school education. Yes, most of them learned about the apostles who lived in the first century or so, but they were also taught that the gift and office of apostle, as well as that of prophet, ceased at the end of the apostolic age.

This is changing. We have now entered a Second Apostolic Age. The form that the Church is taking can be called the "New Apostolic Reformation." I use the word "Reformation" because we are now witnessing the most radical change in the way of doing church since the Protestant Reformation back in the sixteenth century.

## God Creates New Wineskins

Let's apply some biblical language to what we see taking place. We are fortunate enough to have a front row seat as we watch God creating, forming and expanding a major new wineskin for the Church. This is not a new thing for God. As we trace Christian history, it becomes evident that God has constantly been creating new wineskins for His church over the 2,000 years it has been spreading around the world. We shouldn't be surprised that He is doing it again.

The phrase "new wineskins" comes from Matthew 9, when the disciples of John the Baptist came to Jesus. They were upset. One of the things that were upsetting them was that they were hungry—John the Baptist made them fast all the time! They complained that while they were constantly fasting, Jesus' disciples were having a good time eating and drinking! What was going on?

Jesus first explained to them some things concerning the bride and the bridegroom, and then He came to the part about wineskins. He said, "People [do not] put new wine into old wine-skins, or else the wineskins break, the wine is spilled, and the wineskins are ruined. But they put new wine into new wineskins and both are preserved" (Matt. 9:17). Jesus was obviously refer-ring to John the Baptist, the last prominent representative of the Old Covenant. John and his disciples represented what Jesus called an "old wineskin," while Jesus had come to introduce the New Covenant, a "new wineskin."

## Old Wineskins Are Good

It is important to keep in mind that Jesus was not drawing a line between good and bad. Jesus loved John the Baptist. In fact he once said, "Among those born of women, there has not risen one greater than John the Baptist" (Matt. 11:11). In other words, Jesus loved the old wineskin. The only thing about it was that it was not going to receive the new wine.

When we apply this to the New Apostolic Reformation (cur-rently the new wineskin), it helps immensely to keep in mind that the old wineskins (the traditional denominations) are good. God loves them. They were, at one point in time, the new wineskins. When they were, they received God's new wine. But God is no longer pouring His new wine into them, because of His mercy. He loves the old wineskins so much that he doesn't want to ruin them. He wants the traditional denominations to continue to be a blessing to the Body of Christ as long as they possibly can to as many as they possibly can.

## Some May Object

It should neither surprise nor offend us when some old wine-skin Christian leaders raise their voices in objection to the idea that there might be something like a Second Apostolic Age.

After all, they have given their lives to serving God in their traditional denominations or under their traditional mission boards, and have become comfortable with the way these structures operate for the glory of God. There is no question that they have been ministering in God's will and that they should continue to do so. However, the thought of the gift and office of apostle actually operating in the church today understandably pulls them out of their comfort zones, just as much as the lifestyle of Jesus' disciples pulled John the Baptist's disciples out of their comfort zone. Jesus didn't despise them in the least for it.

Jesus also said that to whom much is given, much is required. A good deal of new wine is now being poured into the modern apostolic movement. One of the things this requires is that we assiduously avoid letting the wine go to our heads and thereby come to imagine that we are in some way superior to those yet in old wineskins. This is not so. God will only bless us if we do not let the wine go to our heads in pride and arrogance, but to our hearts, where it will produce the fruit of the Holy Spirit. We must move forward in humility, honoring (while not necessarily imitating) those who have gone before.

The kingdom of God has plenty of room for old wineskins, new wineskins, and those in between.

## Esteeming Each Other

If we do not falter in esteeming each other as Jesus esteemed John the Baptist, God will be able to use all of His people, regardless of their chosen wineskin, to maximize their personal and corporate effectiveness for the advancement of His kingdom around the earth. All will be winners and the nations of the world will be blessed!

# WHAT IS AN APOSTLE?

# A Preliminary Statement
## by C. Peter Wagner, Presiding Apostle,
## International Coalition of Apostles
## (As of May 3, 2006)

The International Coalition of Apostles (ICA), founded in 1999, now counts over 500 members. Membership requires nomination by at least two active ICA members, presuming that peer-level apostles are the most qualified to recognize fellow apostles. This has been mostly a subjective process, given the fact that ICA has not heretofore issued an official statement outlining the basic qualifications expected in a bona fide apostle. Responding to several requests, both inside and outside of ICA, that such a statement be formulated, this paper is a preliminary attempt to respond. I circulated the original draft to all ICA members, and I received two or three dozen very thoughtful responses.

These responses indicate that, after considering the same biblical and phenomenological data, ICA members have arrived at varying conclusions. Consequently, we continue to work toward a general statement that ICA membership can endorse. The ongoing dialog among ICA members as to the details of the profile of an apostle is not unexpected in a young movement such as ours. As we continue, not only will I revise my statement from time to time, but I would also expect that other ICA members will draft statements expressing their point of view. When this happens, those statements will be posted on the ICA website along with this one.

ICA members are in agreement on basic concepts. All agree on the definition of apostle, which is the next item below. This definition is incorporated into the text of the ICA Prospectus, which all potential ICA members sign before joining. Furthermore, all agree that the gifts and offices of apostle and prophet are active in the Church today, just as they were in the Early Church. We will continue to discuss the details as to how these offices operate in the Church. At the moment, therefore, this statement is to be regarded as my personal opinion.

## Definition

An apostle is a Christian leader gifted, taught, commissioned, and sent by God with the authority to establish the foundational government of the Church within an assigned sphere and/or spheres of ministry by hearing what the Spirit is saying to the churches and by setting things in order accordingly for the expansion of the kingdom of God.

## Gifts and Ministries

Apostles, by definition, have been given the spiritual gift of apostle by the grace of God. This gift is listed among many others in 1 Corinthians 12. The same chapter, however, indicates that not all of those with the same gift have the same ministry, and not all those with the same ministry have the same activity (see 1 Cor. 12:4-6).

Many apostles minister primarily in the nuclear church, which traditionally takes the shape of congregations of believers that meet on Sundays or groupings of such congregations, while others minister primarily in the extended church, which is the church in the workplace. These would be termed "nuclear church" apostles, rather than "extended church," or "workplace," apostles.

Some are territorial apostles to whom God has given authority covering a certain geographical area such as a neighborhood, a city, a state or a nation. Others have authority in a certain societal arena such as government or finances or media, etc.

Among those with the gift of apostle, some have the ministry of vertical apostle. This means that they are in an apostolic leadership position over a network of churches and ministries or a network of those who minister in a certain affinity sphere such as women, prayer, youth, worship, etc.

Others are horizontal apostles, who have a ministry of convening and connecting peers such as other apostles or pastors or prophets, etc.

### Gifts and Offices

The gift of apostle, as in the case of all spiritual gifts, is given to believers by God as He pleases (see 1 Cor. 12:11,18). Spiritual gifts are given only by the grace of God.

However, an office, such as the office of apostle, is not given by grace alone, but is given as a result of works that have demonstrated faithfulness in stewardship of the gift. If God has chosen to give a man or woman the gift of apostle, the fruit of that gift will be evident to others, and in due time the Body of Christ will confer the office of apostle on that person. This act is most often termed "commissioning," and it is performed by peer-level apostles, as well as prophets, representing the church, and by laying on hands. The title "apostle" is ordinarily used only by those who have been duly commissioned into the office; although in some situations this principle has not yet been formalized.

### Apostolic Spheres

There is no such thing as an apostle to the whole Church. God assigns to each apostle certain spheres in which he or she exercises authority. Paul makes this clear in 2 Corinthians 10:13-16, where he says, "We, however, will not boast beyond measure, but within the limits of the sphere which God appointed us" (2 Cor. 10:13).

Apostolic spheres can be ecclesiastical, functional, territorial (geographic), cultural or workplace.

## Qualifications of Apostles

Certain qualifications apply to all apostles, regardless of the different ministries or activities that may have been assigned to them by God. These include:

- *Extraordinary character.* Apostles fulfill the leadership requirements outlined in 1 Timothy 3:1-7. They take seriously the warning of James 3:1 that they will be judged with a stricter judgment than most other believers. They are holy (see 1 Pet. 1:15).

- *Humility.* Jesus said that only those who humble themselves will be exalted. Since apostles are exalted by God (see 1 Cor. 12:28), they must be humble in order to qualify.

- *Leadership.* Not all leaders are apostles, but all apostles are leaders. Apostles must have followers to verify their leadership role.

- *Authority.* The characteristic that most distinguishes apostles from other members of the Body of Christ is the authority inherent with the gift of apostle. They gain that authority through fatherhood, not through arrogance or imposition.

- *Integrity.* Apostles are expected to display the integrity that will cause them to be "blameless" (1 Tim. 3:2), and to "have a good testimony among those who are outside" (v. 7).

- *Wisdom.* True apostleship does not come without maturity, and maturity brings wisdom. Apostles have the

God-given ability to see the big picture and to help others find their place in God's plan.

- *Prayer.* While not all apostles would be intercessors per se, all have close contact with God through a disciplined, active and effective prayer life (see Acts 6:4).

## What All Apostles Do

- *They receive revelation.* Apostles hear what the Spirit is saying to the churches. Some of this revelation comes directly to them, some of it is received together with prophets, and some through proper relationships with prophets.

- *They cast vision.* Their vision is based on the revelation they receive.

- *They birth.* Apostles are self-starters who begin new things.

- *They impart.* God uses apostles to activate His blessings in others (see Rom. 1:11).

- *They build.* Apostles strategize and find ways to carry a project along its intended course, including any funding required.

- *They govern.* Apostles are skilled in setting things in order. Along with prophets, they lay the biblical foundation of the Kingdom (see Eph. 2:20).

- *They teach.* Early believers "continued steadfastly in the apostles' teaching" (see Acts 2:42).

- *They send.* Apostles send out those who are equipped to fulfill their role in expanding the kingdom of God.

- *They finish.* Apostles are able to bring a project or a season of God to its desired conclusion. They are uneasy until the project is done. They seldom burn out.

- *They war.* Apostles are the generals in the army of God.

- *They align generations.* Apostles have a long-range perspective on the purposes of God, and they raise up second-tier leadership for the future.

- *They equip.* Apostles equip the saints for the work of the ministry (see Eph. 4:12).

## What Some Apostles Do

Given the differences in temperaments, ministries, callings, activities and geographical locations, many (but not all) apostles will be characterized by:

- Having seen Jesus
- Performing signs and wonders
- Exposing heresy
- Planting new churches
- Imposing church discipline
- Ministering cross-culturally
- Taking back territory from the enemy and converting it to the Kingdom

## Special Characteristics of Workplace Apostles

For the most part, workplace apostles (sometimes referred to as "kings") will be expected to exhibit the same qualifications and move in the same activities as nuclear-church apostles. However, because of their position in the workplace, some sources of their apostolic authority will be somewhat different.

- *Respect.* The starting point for nuclear-church apostles is ordinarily relationships, whereas the starting point for workplace apostles is respect. This means that the authority of nuclear-church apostles is derived largely from their anointing and their relationships. On the other hand, the authority of workplace apostles is derived from the respect they command from others in the workplace, as authenticated by their successful track record. In the workplace, relationships are ordinarily earned through respect, and not vice versa.

- *Money.* A major criterion for respect in the workplace is access to resources, particularly financial resources. Money commands respect, builds credibility, and confers authority more in the workplace than it might in the nuclear church. Money, however, is never the focus; it is regarded only as a necessary tool. Workplace apostles who are financially independent have an advantage over those who are dependent on others for their income.

- *Risk taker.* The road leading to apostolic authority in the workplace is a minefield. Along with the successes, workplace apostles have become accustomed to taking the hits. Most have lost much money and have learned from the experience. However, by God's grace, they fear no one and they do not turn back, because they know that God does not care about money.

- *Renaissance person.* Another criterion for respect is being perceived as a "Renaissance person." These are individuals who have command of a broad spectrum of interests.

• *Negotiating legal structures.* Workplace apostles intuitively move through and around legal entanglements. They do not allow legal structures to set boundaries around what God can do. This is based on inter-workings of relationships built on trust.

• *Position of influence.* Authority also comes from the unusual influence one has in his or her determined sphere of the workplace. The seven molders of culture include: family, religion, government, arts, media, business and education. Each one of these has numerous subdivisions; all have their specific rulebooks as to how influence is attained. Workplace apostles will know what their sphere or spheres are and they will have attained positions of influence within those spheres. The explicit overriding motivation for their use of influence is to glorify God!

• *Kingdom mind-set.* Not every financially successful Christian leader in the workplace is necessarily an apostle. Those who are will also have a Kingdom mentality, meaning that their driving passion is to see God's kingdom values permeate society on every level. They exhibit the expected characteristics of any apostle. They are actively involved in city or nation transformation as well as setting in order the "church" located in the workplace.

• *Commissioning.* (The process for recognizing and commissioning workplace apostles is still under development. ICA will soon come to a consensus as to how this should be done.)

# Scripture Index

# Subject Index

# More of the Best from
# C. Peter Wagner

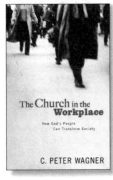

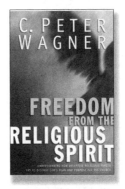
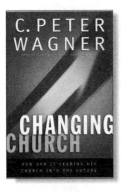

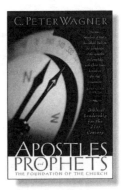

# Now Christians Can Easily Find and Use Their God-Given Spiritual Gifts

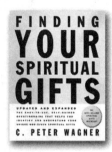

**Your Spiritual Gifts Can Help Your Church Grow**
The Best-Selling Guide for Discovering and Understanding Your Unique Spiritual Gifts and Using them to Bless Others
*C. Peter Wagner*
ISBN 978.08307.36973

**Your Spiritual Gifts Can Help Your Church Grow Small Group Study Guide**
The Easy-to-Use Model for Identifying the Unique Spiritual Gifts of the People in Your Congregation and Applying Their Gifts to Bless Your Community
*C. Peter Wagner*
ISBN 978.08307.36645

**Finding Your Spiritual Gifts**
The Easy-to-Use, Self-Guided Questionnaire That Helps You Identify and Understand Your Unique God-Given Spiritual Gifts
*C. Peter Wagner*
ISBN 978.08307.36942

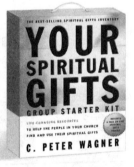

**Discover Your Spiritual Gifts**
The Easy-to-Use Guide That Helps You Identify and Understand Your Unique God-Given Spiritual Gifts
*C. Peter Wagner*
ISBN 978.08307.36782

**Your Spiritual Gifts Group Starter Kit**
Life-Changing Resources to Help the People In Your Church Find and Use Their Spiritual Gifts
*C. Peter Wagner*
ISBN 978.08307.36829

## Available at Bookstores Everywhere!
Visit **www.regalbooks.com** to join **Regal's FREE** e-newsletter. You'll get useful **excerpts from our newest releases** and **special access to online chats with your favorite authors.** Sign up today!

**Regal**
*God's Word for Your World*™
www.regalbooks.com